THEN
HIS VOICE
SHOOK THE EARTH...

THEN
HIS VOICE
SHOOK THE EARTH...

MOUNT SINAI, THE TRUMPET OF GOD, AND THE
RESURRECTION OF THE DEAD IN CHRIST

DAVID W. LOWE
Revised with Foreword by S. Douglas Woodward

CONTENTS

FOREWORD

S. DOUGLAS WOODWARD
AUTHOR OF *DECODING DOOMSDAY* AND *POWER QUEST*

Students of prophecy are in for a treat.

Those of us that study Bible prophecy ardently seek new insights into *eschatology*—the study of 'last things'. We are thrilled when we come across a book that breaks new ground and provides a dramatic and distinctive (yet scriptural) interpretation of the traditional Bible passages addressing future events. David Lowe's *Then His Voice Shook the Earth* is such a book. What the reader will soon learn is, dare I say, revelatory as David provides a breathtaking and novel perspective on the Rapture of the Church and the sequence of events leading up to the Second Coming of Christ. Conventional wisdom would suppose that a book this valuable to the exposition of the Word of Prophecy would be guilty of over-attention to detail—being painstaking in its presentation—not to mention long-winded and unable to hold the readers' attention. But David Lowe does what few authors can do, offering a scholarly approach wedded to a succinct style. Not only is this refreshing, it is powerful. The drama David builds early on when discussing Paul's lonesome journey to Arabia, continues unabated throughout this 160-page study.

Four years ago, I decided it was time for me to write down my views about Bible prophecy. During this period, I authored four books. My first book, *Are We Living in the Last Days?*, was an analysis of the three most essential views that Protestants profess regarding the meaning of the *parousia*—the New Testament's word (almost solely dedicated) to depicting the Lord's coming. In researching the topic (and scouring dozens of titles written during the past decade), I came across David Lowe's *Then His Voice Shook the Earth* and was absolutely astounded. I had not encountered any other prophecy book that opened my eyes to more new insights into rightly dividing the prophetic Word than David's. If you have had a chance to pick up my first book, you might recall that I referred to David's insights numerous times. No doubt, much of the thunder echoing forth from my comments resulted by stealing some of David's.

In fact, being somewhat of a scholar on the Second Coming, I can say without much fear of contradiction that no book on the Apocalypse provides more value to the task of explaining the Book of Revelation and the Rapture of the Church than *Then His Voice Shook the Earth*. In fact, I had not read any book on Bible prophecy that personally influenced my thinking as much as David's since I first read the grandfather of all modern prophetic books, Hal Lindsey's *Late Great Planet Earth*. Yes, I had read many books written by Tim LaHaye, Grant Jeffrey, Chuck Missler, and many other outstanding Christian authors. They are wonderful and invaluable aids to our understanding of Bible prophecy. But none of these great authors had ever provided me as many crucial insights into biblical eschatology in a single book as did David. And all of that value in a 160-page work. Amazing! But is my praise overstated? Not if you subscribe to a premillennial point of view regarding the Lord's return. Allow me to cite three particular instances where David's work cracks the code on Bible prophecy.

First, the identity of the trumpet of God. What is this ominous trumpet? Is it the Shofar that is blown 100 times on Rosh Hashanah? Is this the seventh of Seven Trumpets referenced in Revelation chapters 8 through 11? We read that the final, seventh trumpet is sounded in Revelation 11:15, "And the seventh angel sounded [his trumpet]; and there were great voices in heaven, saying, 'The kingdoms of this world are become the kingdoms of our Lord, and of his Christ; and he shall reign for ever and ever.'" Is this final trumpet of Revelation 'the last trump?' Or could the 'last trump' be something else? David believes it is indeed a different trumpet than mentioned by John in his vision. And once we understand the true nature of that trumpet, what we learn dramatically changes our interpretation of the famous Pauline references in I Corinthians 15:2 ("In a flash, in the twinkling of an eye, at the last trumpet. For the trumpet will sound, the dead will be raised imperishable, and we will be changed"); as well as I Thessalonians 4:16-17 ("For the Lord himself will come down from heaven, with a loud command, with the voice of the archangel and with the trumpet call of God, and the dead in Christ will rise first. After that, we who are still alive and are left will be caught up together with them in the clouds to meet the Lord in the air. And so we will be with the Lord forever"). Few subjects in Bible prophecy have caused more debate than the identity of this trumpet. As you will soon see, David provides what I believe is the most biblically sound solution to this most puzzling of apocalyptic controversies.

Once this issue is resolved, we see it opens the possibility for a completely new, and (in my experience) distinctive chronology of the massive events detailed in Revelation 4-7. The interpretation offered by *Then His Voice Shook the Earth* offers a far more compelling sequence of events than the traditional dispensational understanding, an interpretation proffered by no less a scholar than Dr. John F. Walvoord, the standard-setter for dispensational interpretations. Indeed, Lindsey, LaHaye, Jeffrey, and almost all other dispensational authors have settled on Walvoord's 'standard' interpretation which sees the 'Four Horsemen of the Apocalypse' appearing at the outset of the 'Great Tribulation.' But what if these horsemen appear before the Tribulation begins? What if the first horsemen appeared 2,000 years before the Tribulation begins? Suffice it to say, the reader will be astounded by the biblical exposition David provides. His point of view shows a tight correlation between Christ's teaching in the Olivet Discourse (See Matthew 24) and the vision of John as recorded in Revelation.

And finally, at least in my quick summary, there is the whole issue of earthquakes tied to resurrections. David connects the dots in a most remarkable way. After I read his argument, I was blown away by the recounting of numerous scriptures I had never linked before and how they lead to a conclusion about what must happen at the resurrection of the Saints—a conclusion that will shake the reader up (if you pardon the pun). This insight alone is worth the price of the book! Indeed, the implications of his suggestion are staggering. While it is true that we cannot be dogmatic about the physical impact upon the world when the resurrection of the dead occurs (and David isn't), the possibility he proposes has substantial biblical support. And it resolves some deep-seated difficulties in reconciling certain events outlined in Revelation.

Given what I know about David, it isn't surprising that the Lord has opened His word to him, granting him such original insights into the mystery of the Rapture and the circumstances surrounding the Second Coming. As a lad, David put to memory much of the New Testament. He knows the Word intimately and his knowledge shines forth in both his biblical approach as well as his person (experienced through numerous, enjoyable long-distance conversations). David regards the Bible as a sacred book—nothing is placed between its covers by accident. All details are important to rightly understand the Lord's meaning. He believes, as do I, that the Lord speaks to us through every word. We both fervently affirm that when we take this approach to the Bible, not only do we treat it with respect, we regard it a living book able to teach us afresh regarding the will of God—serving not just as a sourcebook of information, but as a practical guide for living. It is a lamp unto our feet (Psalm 119:105, Proverbs 6:23). After you read *Then His Voice Shook the Earth*, not only you will witness this sparkling light firsthand, but your anticipation about the soon return of Jesus Christ for His Saints will be rekindled!

May you feel the excitement I experienced when I first read *Then His Voice Shook the Earth*. Maranatha!

S. Douglas Woodward
Woodinville, Washington
January 2012

AUTHOR'S PREFACE

The main purpose of this book is to emphasize an important event that is often overlooked within the modern eschatological genre, and that is the resurrection of the dead in Christ, but more specifically, its impact on the earth's surface. Too often, the catching-up event, or rapture, has received the lion's share of the attention without giving due consideration to what impact the simultaneous resurrection of millions, perhaps billions, of believers throughout the centuries will have on the earth. While the catching-up event is an important conclusion to the process of the translation of believers, the resurrection of the dead, at the sounding of the trumpet of God, will precede that event and profoundly impact the global landscape.

Consideration of this global impact led to my first book, *Earthquake Resurrection*, and now *Then His Voice Shook the Earth*, a more compact version of that work which includes important new information. The topic is fascinating and I find the merits of the model to be quite compelling. I believe that scholars, pastors, teachers, and laypersons will all greatly benefit from this important study. While I consider the foremost calling of the believer to be daily personal evangelism by calling the lost to repentance, an informed understanding of the prophetic scriptures is an important part of an overall witness of the gospel. The catastrophic resurrection model explained in this book will equip every believer with a solid understanding of what will occur at the powerful future resurrection of the dead in Christ, the next major event on the prophetic calendar.

Useful Points of Reference

The reader is encouraged to keep the following points in mind as progression is made through the book:

- While the use of the terms "rapture" and "tribulation period" are commonly understood among those who study Bible prophecy, these two concepts will be referred to as "the catching-up" and "the day of the Lord's wrath," respectively, throughout the book.
- Scripture quotations, unless otherwise noted, are from the New English Translation of the Bible (NET). The scripture is quoted by permission, copyright © 2003 Biblical Studies Press, L.L.C.
- Hebrew, Greek, and Latin words and phrases have been presented in their transliterated form rather than in the original language form, and in *italicized* font.
- Although the author of the epistle to the Hebrews is not identified in the epistle, based upon the best internal and external evidence about its authorship, it has been assumed in this book that the author of Hebrews was the apostle Paul.

I would like to acknowledge several people who have helped in the development of this project, either knowingly or unknowingly. Tony Burtovoy, you have been a great source of information and ideas in the realm of current events and eschatology. Peter Goodgame, thank you for being obedient to the Lord and writing Red Moon Rising. Cory Ferguson, you have again been a big help with the cover and artwork, and a source of encouragement in the Lord. Robert Tanner, David

Molina, and Larry Shuck, thank you for your interest in my projects and for helping me to get the message out. Robert Tanner, thank you for your hospitality in Alaska and the opportunity to present the model to your congregation. Steve Gregg, thank you for your teaching from which I have learned so much over the last year. Finally, thanks to all who read *Earthquake Resurrection*, who provided feedback, and who recommended it to others. I have developed friendships with many of you that will be cherished for a lifetime.

It is my sincere prayer that the information in this book has a profound spiritual impact on you. This certainly was the case for me in researching and writing it. May it challenge and inspire you to search the Word of God as if you were searching for hidden treasure, and cause you to cherish the selfless sacrifice of my Lord and Savior like never before.

David W. Lowe
Wichita, KS
November 2006

* * *

ADDENDUM for 2nd Edition

In 2011, I was privileged to become acquainted with Doug Woodward, a premier author and Bible scholar. I have been blessed to read Doug's work, including *Are We Living in the Last Days* and his latest effort, *Power Quest*. Doug encouraged me to produce a 2nd edition of this book, and blessed me with the Foreword included herein. I am honored to be associated with Doug, and I strongly encourage you to become familiar with his inspiring story and all of his great books, which both glorify the Lord and expound on the prophetic scriptures with inspired precision. Thank you, Doug!

David W. Lowe
Wichita, KS
February 2012

SECTION I

THE RESURRECTION AND THE LAST TRUMPET

1

THE MYSTERIOUS ARABIAN CONNECTION

M ysteries. For some, the word may evoke thoughts of fear and wonder; for others, thoughts of supernatural dimensions and heavenly beings. Mysteries are what the apostle Paul oftentimes said he was revealing to the readers of his epistles. What was the source of the mysteries? It was a direct special revelation from Jesus Christ. In his letters to the believers of the churches of Galatia and Ephesus, this truth served as an important foundation for what he wanted to convey:

> Now I want you to know, brothers and sisters, that the gospel I preached is not of human origin. For I did not receive it or learn it from any human source; instead I received it by a revelation of Jesus Christ. (*Gal 1:11-12*)

> To me—less than the least of all the saints—this grace was given, to proclaim to the Gentiles the unfathomable riches of Christ and to enlighten

everyone about God's secret plan [*mustérion*]—a
secret that has been hidden for ages in God who
has created all things. (*Eph 3:8-9*)

Paul was chosen by the Lord to be a conduit through which
God's secret plan, hidden for many ages, could be revealed. His
use of *mustérion* is common throughout his epistles, by which he
intimated that what he was revealing was something which, prior
to his writing, had not been understood. One of the mysteries
Paul revealed in his epistles is the three-stage process of the
translation of the bodies of believers, consisting of:

1. Resurrection of the dead in Christ. (I Cor 15:51-52; I The
   4:16-17)
2. Transformation of the perishable bodies of all believers into
   imperishable bodies. (Phi 3:21; I Cor 15:51-52)
3. Catching up of all believers into the air to meet the Lord,
   including both the resurrected dead in Christ and remaining
   living believers. (I The 4:16-17)

The powerful catastrophic *effect* that this mysterious three-
stage translation process will have on the earth, with an
emphasis on the resurrection to immortality, is the focus of this
book.

The Mysterious Arabian Connection

Most are familiar with the encounter Saul of Tarsus ("Paul" after
his conversion) experienced with Jesus Christ on the Road to
Damascus, during which he spoke directly to Saul from heaven.
But here is a key question to be understood: was it during this
encounter that Paul received what he later referred to as the
revelation of mysteries from Jesus Christ?

Much detail is provided regarding what happened to Saul on
the Road to Damascus, and it seems from Luke's description in

Acts chapter 9 and from Paul's descriptions of the experience later in the same book, that the encounter was a relatively brief one. After a short dialogue with Jesus, Saul was instructed to continue on into the city.

So, when did Paul receive his revelation directly from Jesus Christ, if not on the Road to Damascus? Twice in his first epistle to the Corinthians, Paul revealed that he had personally met with Jesus:

> Am I not free? Am I not an apostle? Have I not seen Jesus our Lord? Are you not my work in the Lord? (*I Cor 9:1*)

> Last of all, as though to one born at the wrong time, he [Jesus Christ] appeared to me also. (*I Cor 15:8*)

According to these verses, Paul claimed to have seen Jesus Christ in a *physical*, resurrected form. I do not believe Paul was referring to what happened on the Road to Damascus in these verses because he saw a bright light and was blinded. How can a blind man claim to see anything or anyone and expect to be believed? When later recounting the Damascus Road experience before King Agrippa in Acts chapter 26, Paul said that the Lord told him he would appear to him again *in the future*:

> But get up and stand on your feet, for I have appeared to you for this reason, to designate you in advance as a servant and witness to the things you have seen and to the things in which I will appear to you. (*Act 26:16*)

It is true that the Lord appeared to Paul at least three times during his journeys described in Acts. In Corinth, the Lord appeared to him in a vision (18:9-11); in his defense at the temple in Jerusalem, Paul said he saw the Lord while in a trance (22:18); and after his brief appearance before the Jewish Sanhedrin council, the Lord stood near to Paul and told him that he would not die in Jerusalem, but would be going to Rome (23:11). If any of these three instances would qualify as the *physical* appearance of the Lord to which he was referring, the third would be the best choice, as the first two appearances were in a trance or vision-state.

However, according to Paul's words recorded in Acts chapter 26, the Lord, speaking to him on the Road to Damascus before his conversion to Christianity, was going to appear to him in the future to designate him as a servant and witness of things he would later show him. The Jerusalem appearance of reassurance about reaching Rome lacks these important elements, and takes place long after his conversion and revelation of the mysteries in his epistles. It seems, then, that Paul must have been referring to a much more substantive physical appearance, in the early years of his ministry, when maintaining that he had seen the risen Jesus Christ.

After his conversion and restoration of sight in Damascus, Paul revealed in his letter to the Galatians that he made an inexplicable journey to Arabia:

> But when the one who set me apart from birth and called me by his grace was pleased to reveal his Son in me so that I could preach him among the Gentiles, I did not go to ask advice from any human being, nor did I go up to Jerusalem to see those who were apostles before me, but right away I departed to Arabia, and then returned to Damascus. (*Gal 1:15-17*)

According to Acts chapter 9, Saul was led blind into Damascus, there received his sight, and then stayed in Damascus for several days. There is no reference in that chapter about a long journey to Arabia, and so it is difficult to incorporate into the historical narrative of Acts chapter 9. The most likely spot is between verses 25 and 26, when Luke wrote that Paul returned to Jerusalem for the first time since his conversion.

According to his testimony in Galatians chapter 1 above, before he went to Jerusalem to meet the apostles, Paul left for Arabia, then came to Jerusalem three years later. It is therefore agreed among most scholars that Paul split these three years between the initial stay in Damascus and his sojourn in Arabia.

Arabia is mentioned but twice in the New Testament, excluding the reference to "Arabians" in Acts 2:11, and both are in Paul's Galatian epistle. After stating that he visited Arabia in the first chapter, he stated in the fourth chapter that Mount Sinai is in Arabia:

> Now Hagar represents Mount Sinai in Arabia and corresponds to the present Jerusalem, for she is in slavery with her children. (*Gal 4:25*)

Why did Paul feel it was necessary to tell the Galatian readers that he went to Arabia while in the midst of justifying his supernatural, heavenly commission to preach the gospel? What part did this mysterious journey to Arabia play in his immediate post-conversion experience such that he felt compelled to include it in the list of places he went?

The answer to this question is illuminating in our quest to understand Paul's revelation of the mystery of the future resurrection of the dead in Christ. For Paul, a journey to Arabia was important because Mount Sinai was located there, the one location on the earth in which God came down in fire to communicate the first covenant with his Hebrew ancestors, in a geographic area that is currently in the territory of modern Saudi Arabia.[1] And in the narrative of the Mount Sinai appearance, I believe Paul was shown by the Lord a pattern for the mystery of the resurrection of the dead in Christ.

In the Footsteps of Elijah

Ideas for the reasons why Paul was compelled to make a long journey to Arabia after his conversion have ranged a desire to experience a time of meditation in solitude to prepare for what the Lord had commissioned him to do, to his initial attempt to evangelize those in the area around the desert of Damascus, such as the Nabateans. Perhaps the Lord instructed him to go to Arabia after the Damascus Road experience? Unfortunately, there are scant clues in scripture to support these ideas. A more plausible explanation for the Arabia visit has been proposed by Dr. N. Thomas Wright, the Bishop of Durham, United Kingdom. Dr. Wright proposed that both Paul's pre-conversion persecution of Christians to the death, and his post-conversion journey to Arabia, were patterned after the life of Elijah the prophet. Following in the footsteps of Elijah, who like him was extremely zealous for the Lord, would mean that he would need to make a journey to Arabia, to the mountain of the Lord, where Elijah met with the Lord and received a new prophetic commission.[2]

After telling the Galatian readers that he received his gospel by a revelation of Jesus Christ, Paul made reference to his past life in Judaism, and stressed that he was following in the *zealous* tradition of the ancestors:

> For you have heard of my former way of life in Judaism, how I was savagely persecuting the church of God and trying to destroy it. I was advancing in Judaism beyond many of my contemporaries in my nation, and was extremely zealous for the traditions of my ancestors. (*Gal 1:13-14*)

18

Prior to his conversion, Saul's zeal was certainly not restricted to Torah head knowledge or prayer. Just like his ancestors, Saul felt it was his duty to put to death Jews who were shunning the God of Israel by following after other religions. He savagely persecuted the church with the intent of completely destroying it, and he voted against Christians in sentencing them to death.

Saul was following in the zealous tradition of Elijah. Under King Ahab's rule, Israel had fallen further into worship of Baal than it ever had before. At Mount Carmel, Elijah called on the Lord to prove he was the true God, and he delivered with fire from heaven. In response to this miracle, Elijah had the 450 prophets of Baal seized, led into the Kidron Valley, and executed. After this victorious event, Jezebel vowed to kill Elijah, so he fled for his life to Beer Sheba. Dejected and disillusioned, Elijah was led from there to Mount Sinai, where he met the Lord and declared his zeal to him after this 40-day journey:

> He answered, "I have been absolutely loyal [qânâ'] to the LORD, the sovereign God, even though the Israelites have abandoned the agreement they made with you, torn down your altars, and killed your prophets with the sword. I alone am left and now they want to take my life." (*I Kin 19:14*)

Elijah said he had been absolutely loyal, or zealous (*qânâ'*) toward God in the midst of a rebellious Israelite nation, but nonetheless found himself in grave danger. But in his acutely downtrodden state, Elijah at Mount Sinai received instruction and encouragement from the Lord. Paul made reference to Elijah's Mount Sinai encounter in Romans chapter 11, comparing those 7,000 whom the Lord had called out as a remnant in the time of Elijah to the remnant of believers chosen by grace.

But it is very important to notice where the Lord instructed Elijah to go from Mount Sinai in Arabia:

> The LORD said to him, "Go back the way you came and then head for the Desert of Damascus. Go and anoint Hazael king over Syria. (*I Kin 9:15*)

Just as Elijah was instructed to return from Arabia to Damascus, so Paul in Galatians 1:17 revealed that after making his visit to Arabia, he returned to Damascus! This is a very important clue in establishing a case that Paul traveled to Mount Sinai to follow in the footsteps of Elijah and attempt to encounter the Lord on the sacred and historic mountain of God.

Similar to story of Elijah, Saul's may have also justified his persecutory actions against his fellow countrymen by following in the zealous tradition of Phinehas. This bold man showed his zeal for the Lord by killing one of his own Israelite brethren who was having sexual relations with a Moabite woman. The rebellious Israelites were participating in ritual sexual immorality with the Moabite women in the worship of Baal, according to Numbers chapter 25. The Lord called Phinehas' violent zeal an act of atonement for the Israelites:

> "Phinehas son of Eleazar, the son of Aaron the priest, has turned my anger away from the Israelites when he manifested such zeal for my sake among them, so that I did not consume the Israelites in my zeal. So it will be to him and his descendants after him a covenant of a permanent priesthood, because he has been zealous [*qânâ'*]

for his God, and has made atonement for the Israelites." (*Num 25:11; 13*)

Saul could justify his persecutory actions as similar acts of cleansing or atonement, because his rebellious countrymen were following a new way which claimed to follow the one true God, but was contrary to the traditions of his ancestors. He acted well within the purview of the tradition of Phineas, in his view, in persecuting and destroying Jews who had converted to Christianity. Just like Phinehas and Elijah, his tremendous zeal for the law of the Lord drove him to eradicate those whom he viewed as idolaters, no better than worshippers of Baal. But the Damascus Road experience changed all that, and his zeal for the Lord was redirected to preaching repentance toward God and faith toward the Lord Jesus Christ.[3]

A Pattern Revealed at Mount Sinai

Before this, however, he followed the model of Elijah by traveling to Arabia where Mount Sinai was located, the mountain where Moses and Elijah met the Lord. A journey from Damascus to Mount Sinai is not a short one, at approximately 340 miles, but it certainly isn't unprecedented. For example, as discussed earlier, after Elijah traveled 40 days from Beer Sheba to Mount Sinai, the Lord instructed him to return from the mountain to the Desert of Damascus. Paul had already made a trip of approximately 130 miles from Jerusalem to Damascus to arrest Christians, so it would not be out of the question for him to make this journey to Arabia, especially given that Elijah, the prophet after whom he modeled his zeal for the Lord, made a journey of equal distance from Mount Sinai to Damascus.

Just as Elijah received a renewed prophetic commission at Mount Sinai, it is reasonable to conclude that Paul received details on his new commission from Jesus Christ at Mount Sinai in Arabia, which included revelation about the mysteries of the church revealed in his epistles. Such an Arabian experience becomes even more intriguing in light of the similarities between the events on Mount Sinai when the Ten Commandments were given to Moses and Paul's revelation of the future sudden catching up of believers, including:

1. Moses was instructed to sanctify the people and have them wash their clothes (Exodus 19:10). Similarly, a person must be sanctified and washed in order to be a believer who will be resurrected and caught up.
2. The Lord descended onto Mount Sinai from the heavens (Exodus 19:18). Similarly, Paul stated that the Lord will descend from heaven before the resurrection of the dead in Christ.
3. The appearance of the Lord on Mount Sinai was accompanied by the trumpet sound of God's voice (Exodus 19:19). Similarly, Paul stated that the Lord's future coming will be accompanied by the trumpet of God.
4. Moses was summoned to the top of the mountain by the Lord, and he went up and met the Lord (Exodus 19:20). Similarly, Paul stated that believers will be suddenly caught up together into the air to meet the Lord.

A revelation of the Lord's mysterious future descent to catch up believers was not the only revelation Paul received at Mount Sinai. There is another fascinating connection between the events on Mount Sinai experienced by Moses and the children of Israel, and the future resurrection of the dead in Christ. This connection, nestled within Paul's description of the original Mount Sinai events in Hebrews chapter 12, and his description of the resurrection of the dead in Christ in I Corinthians chapter 15, is a future shaking of the heavens and the earth by the trumpet voice of the Lord.

---

[1] There is convincing evidence that Mount Sinai has been discovered in modern-day Saudi Arabia at a location called Jabal al-Lawz, not at the traditional Sinai Peninsula site. Two books, *In Search of the Mountain of God: The Discovery of the Real Mt. Sinai* by Robert Cornuke and *The Exodus Case: New Discoveries Confirm the Historical Exodus* by Lennart Möeller, detail this evidence and provide eyewitness accounts that the top of Jabal al-Lawz, Arabic for "Mountain of Almonds," is completely charred and burnt black. These men relied on both the ancient scriptures and archaeological evidence in meticulously mapping a more accurate route of the Israelites from Egypt to this mountain range in Arabia.

[2] Wright, N. Thomas (1996). "Paul, Arabia, and Elijah (Galatians 1:17)," *Journal of Biblical Literature*, vol. 115, pp. 683-692.

[3] The entire section discussing the zeal of the ancestors serving as a model for Paul's pre-Damascus worldview must be attributed to N. Thomas Wright, cited above, as well as Martin Hengel's, *The Zealots: Investigations into the Jewish Freedom Movement in the Period from Herod I until 70 A.D.*, Edinburgh: Clark, published in 1961.

2

THEN HIS VOICE SHOOK THE
EARTH . . .

According to I Corinthians 15:51-52, the simultaneous resurrection and transformation event which begins the process of the translation of the bodies of believers will be set in motion by the sounding of a trumpet, which Paul termed the "last trumpet," or *eschatēi sálpiggi* in Greek:

> Listen, I will tell you a mystery: We will not all sleep, but we will all be changed — in a moment, in the blinking of an eye, at the last trumpet [*eschatēi sálpiggi*]. For the trumpet will sound, and the dead will be raised imperishable, and we will be changed. (*I Cor 15:51-52*)

This passage adds detail to his initial disclosure of this future event in his first epistle to the Thessalonians. In that letter, he revealed:

> For the Lord himself will come down from
> heaven with a shout of command, with the voice
> of the archangel, and with the trumpet [*sálpiggi*]
> of God, and the dead in Christ will rise first. Then
> we who are alive, who are left, will be suddenly
> caught up together with them in the clouds to
> meet the Lord in the air. And so we will always
> be with the Lord. (*I The 4:16-17*)

There are at least four points of congruence between Paul's
description of the resurrection of the dead in I Corinthians
15:51-52 and in I Thessalonians 4:16-17 which have led students
of the Bible to conclude that Paul was describing the same event:

1. Both passages reveal that the dead in Christ, believers who
   have died throughout history, will be resurrected.
2. Both passages reveal that there will be a trumpet sound that
   immediately precedes this resurrection of the dead.
3. Both passages reveal that there will be a separate group of
   believers who have not died, but are alive and remaining at
   this future resurrection event.
4. Both passages reveal a supernatural act will be performed
   upon those alive and remaining believers at the time of, or
   just after, the resurrection of the dead.

It is abundantly clear from these points of congruence that
Paul was referring to the same event within the two passages.
Therefore, it can be reasonably concluded that the "last trumpet"
sounding prior to the resurrection of the dead referred to in I
Corinthians 15:52 is the same as the "trumpet of God" sounding
prior to the resurrection of the dead referred to in I
Thessalonians 4:16. Notice that the Greek noun for trumpet in
both passages is *sálpiggi*. According to Strong's Concordance,
sálpigx is derived from several different words which are all

used in the New Testament to describe motion, shaking, billowing, or reverberation. The Greek *seismós*, a violent shaking or earthquake, is derived from the primary verb *seíō*, which has its roots in *sálpigx*.

The Trumpet of God and His Voice

What did Paul mean, then, by the term "trumpet of God?" Does the idea of God Almighty blowing a literal ram's horn or golden trumpet come to mind? Given his omnipotence, the image of the Creator of the universe placing a literal trumpet to his mouth in heaven or on earth seems a bit contrived. Could it be that the trumpet of God is actually his voice rather than a trumpet placed to his mouth and blown?

Fortunately, there is a wealth of scripture that will shed light on this important question. The first to be examined is Exodus chapter 19, in which the scene is set for the dispensation of the Ten Commandments. This incredible event featured the living God revealing his presence in our three-dimensional world, in fact, coming down on Mount Sinai in Arabia under the cover of a dense cloud, with thunder, lightning, fire, earthquakes, and a long and loud trumpet sound. The Lord gave Moses specific instructions for this event, including setting up boundaries to keep the people away from the mountain, how the people should prepare themselves for the event, and when he would come down to speak with him and reveal himself to the people.

When the Lord came down on the third day, the people saw the fire, the cloud, and the smoke, and were terrified. But they also *heard* something very important: what in Hebrew was described as the "voice of the trumpet," or *qôl shôphâr* :

> And it came to pass on the third day in the morning, that there were thunders and lightnings, and a thick cloud upon the mount, and the voice of the trumpet [*qôl shôphâr*] exceeding loud; so

that all the people that was in the camp trembled. (*Exo 19:16 KJV*)

A verse later in the narrative provides more detail about the voice, or sound, of the trumpet that was heard:

> And when the voice of the trumpet [*qôl shôphâr*] sounded long, and waxed louder and louder, Moses spake, and God answered him by a voice [*qôl*]. (*Exo 19:19 KJV*)

Here it is revealed just what the sound of the trumpet, or *qôl shôphâr*, was: God communicating vocally with Moses. There are several other scriptures which corroborate this conclusion, including:

> And all the people saw the thunderings, and the lightnings, and the noise of the trumpet [*qôl shôphâr*], and the mountain smoking: and when the people saw it, they removed, and stood afar off. And they said unto Moses, Speak thou with us, and we will hear: but let not God speak with us, lest we die. (*Exo 20:18-19 KJV*)

The people were mortified by the thought of God's voice speaking to them again. They would have rather had Moses speak with them than God. When these events were later recalled in Deuteronomy chapters 4 and 5, the Lord's voice was again connected to the event:

> Then the LORD spoke to you from the middle of the fire; you heard speech [*qôl*] but you could not see anything — only a voice [*qôl*] was heard. (*Deu 4:12*)

> The LORD said these things to your entire
> assembly at the mountain from the middle of the
> fire, the cloud, and the darkness with a loud voice
> [qôl], and that was all he said. (*Deu 5:22a*)

This important Mount Sinai event was also described in the
New Testament. In Hebrews chapter 12, Paul provided
corroboration for the voice of the Lord being associated with the
reverberating sound of a trumpet. In contrasting the first
covenant established through Moses with the new covenant
established through Jesus Christ, Paul described the scene on
Mount Sinai as follows:

> For you have not come to something that can be
> touched, to a burning fire and darkness and gloom
> and a whirlwind and the blast of a trumpet and a
> voice uttering words such that those who heard
> begged to hear no more. (*Heb 12:18-19*)

Paul explained that the blast of the trumpet was associated
with the voice that was uttering words, meaning God's voice
speaking *was* the trumpet blast heard in Mount Sinai. This is
solid support for the Exodus chapter 19 description of the
trumpet blast yielding a voice uttering words, a voice which the
people begged to stop because it was extremely loud, but more
importantly for the sake of this study, because it shook the
surrounding landscape.

It should be clear, then, that the Lord possesses a voice that
manifests with the force of a loud, reverberating trumpet sound.
Indeed, John was witness to this on the Isle of Patmos when he
twice heard the voice of the Lord speaking to him with the sound
of a trumpet (Revelation 1:10 and 4:1). This is not the only form
that his voice can take, for Elijah heard the still, soft voice of the
Lord in a cave of the same mountain, Mount Sinai. As will be

revealed, however, God has reserved his trumpet voice for one final shaking of the earth and the heavens.

The Trumpet Voice of God Shook the Earth

In both Job chapter 37 and Psalm chapter 29, the voice of the Lord is described as powerful and thundering, with the ability to shake the earth in a violent manner. While these passages are perhaps partially poetic, the message cannot be mistaken: the power of the voice of the Lord when it is sounded within our three-dimensional world. Another important piece of the Mount Sinai narrative in which this power was on display is the description of the scene when the Lord descended and began to speak with Moses:

> And mount Sinai was altogether on a smoke, because the LORD descended upon it in fire: and the smoke thereof ascended as the smoke of a furnace, and the whole mount quaked greatly. And when the voice of the trumpet sounded long, and waxed louder and louder, Moses spake, and God answered him by a voice. (*Exo 19:18-19 KJV*)

Here it is revealed that when the entire Sinai mountain region was shaking in a violent manner as the Lord descended on it, the voice of the trumpet was sounding long. Clearly, this was a violent shaking of Mount Sinai. Consider the Psalmist's description of the scene:

> O God, when thou wentest forth before thy people, when thou didst march through the wilderness; Selah: The earth shook, the heavens also dropped at the presence of God: even Sinai

itself was moved at the presence of God, the God
of Israel. (*Psa 68:7-8 KJV*)

Here, the exodus from Egypt is described as the "march
through the wilderness," when the people of God were led to
Mount Sinai. The earth was described as experiencing a shaking,
and the mountains were moved in the presence of God.
Admittedly, it is not clear from these passages whether the
quaking of the mountain range was because of the descent of the
Lord in fire, or the voice of the trumpet sounding, or both.
However, Paul's conclusion about the Mount Sinai events in
Hebrews chapter 12 leaves no doubt as to what caused the
shaking on Mount Sinai when he descended upon it in fire. The
first clause of Hebrews 12:26 reveals the answer:

Then his voice shook the earth . . . (*Heb 12:26(a)*)

What is the "then" to which Paul was referring? It was the
scene he had just described in verses 18-21, a scene so terrifying
that Moses himself shuddered with fear. With Hebrews 12:26(a),
Paul confirms that the supernatural catalyst for the shaking of
the earth at Mount Sinai was the trumpet voice of the Lord.
Then, at Mount Sinai, his voice was the cause of the shaking of
the earth; it could not be any more clearly stated than that. As
previously established, the voice of the Lord sounded like a
trumpet reverberating when blown, yet he was uttering words,
speaking to Moses.

The "Last Trumpet" and the "Once More" of Hebrews 12:26(b)

Therefore, it is clear that (a) the "last trumpet" is equivalent to
the "trumpet of God," (b) this trumpet of God will be sounded
just before the resurrection of the dead in Christ, and (c) the
trumpet of God is his voice uttering words, and when sounded, it

shakes the earth. In the final clause of Hebrews 12:26, Paul revealed the key to understanding the meaning of the last trumpet which will sound before the future resurrection of the dead in Christ and the catching up.

After explaining that the trumpet voice of God shook the earth at Mount Sinai, Paul made a chilling announcement about the next time–the last time–that it will shake not only the earth, but also the heavens:

> Then his voice shook the earth, but now he has promised, "I will once more shake not only the earth but heaven too." (*Heb 12:26*)

From an initial reading of this verse, it can be concluded that (a) God's voice shook the earth at Mount Sinai, (b) once again, God's trumpet voice will shake the earth, as well as the heavens, and (c) this will be the *last time* God's trumpet voice shakes the earth and heavens. Yes, one last time: the *last trumpet* voice of God. In this verse, Paul was quoting a prophecy written by the Old Testament prophet Haggai when stating that God promised "I will once more shake not only the earth but heaven too." Notice also that Haggai connects his prophecy to the exodus from Egypt and a promise the Lord made to them at Mount Sinai:

> 'Do not fear, because I made a promise to your ancestors when they left Egypt, and my spirit even now testifies to you.' Moreover, the LORD who rules over all says: 'In just a little while I will once again shake the sky and the earth, the sea and the dry ground. (*Hag 2:5-6*)

This prophecy confirms the conclusions drawn about the passage from Hebrews above: that God at Mount Sinai shook the earth with his powerful trumpet voice, and that it will once more shake the earth and the heavens at some point in the future.

From the phrase "once more," two very important conclusions can be logically drawn. First, that something took place in the past, at least once, and second, that it is going to take place exactly one more time. The "last trumpet" fits the "once more" description perfectly, because the trumpet of God's voice shook the earth once in the past (Mount Sinai), and will do so one last time (the resurrection of the dead in Christ).

This alleviates longstanding confusion about the meaning of the last trumpet in supposed equation with the seventh trumpet blown by an angel in Revelation chapter 11. This seventh trumpet is not the trumpet of God, but rather the trumpet of an angel. In addition, the seven trumpet judgments were a revelation given to John, not Paul who wrote to the Corinthian church many years before John's Revelation.

Given Paul's background in Old Testament scripture and Jewish customs, he clearly understood what happened on Mount Sinai, that God's trumpet voice was the cause of the shaking of the earth at that time, and to what the prophet Haggai was referring when he wrote that the Lord would once more shake the earth and the heavens. It is apparent that Paul intimated this knowledge to the Corinthians when he visited them, and explained the connections of the trumpet voice of God and the last trumpet, so that an explanation in I Corinthians 15:52 was not necessary for the readers. Fortunately, all the pieces to the mystery are available for us in the Word, allowing us to exegete exactly what Paul meant. In using the term, "last trumpet," he was guiding future readers, through the Holy Spirit, to use the information in Exodus, Haggai, and his first letter to the Thessalonians to understand that it will be God's trumpet voice sounding at the resurrection of the dead in Christ, shaking the earth and the heavens.

The next question to ask is where, within the chronology of Revelation, would the resurrection of the dead fit within the description of a massive shaking of both the earth and the heavens. The event must precede both the day of God's wrath and the appearance of resurrected and caught-up believers in heaven. Such an event is described within Revelation in the events which take place at the opening of the sixth seal:

> Then I looked when the Lamb opened the sixth seal, and a huge earthquake took place; the sun became as black as sackcloth made of hair, and the full moon became blood red; and the stars in the sky fell to the earth like a fig tree dropping its unripe figs when shaken by a fierce wind. The sky was split apart like a scroll being rolled up, and every mountain and island was moved from its place. (*Rev 6:12-14*)

In this passage, there is clearly a shaking of both the earth (a huge earthquake; mountains and islands move) and the heavens (the sun; the moon; the stars in the sky; the sky itself). In addition, the events of the sixth seal will take place before the day of the Lord's wrath, which allows for the three-stage translation of believers prior to the pouring out of the Lord's wrath on the earth.

Connecting the events of the post-exodus Mount Sinai experience, Haggai's prophecy of God's voice "once more" shaking both the earth and the heavens, and Paul's association of these two passages in Hebrews chapter 12, a startling conclusion can be drawn. The "last trumpet" is a reference to the trumpet voice of God sounding once more in the future, at the resurrection of the dead in Christ, shaking the earth and the heavens in fulfillment of the prophecy of Haggai.

Now Paul's journey to Mount Sinai, in the footsteps of his ancestral mentor Elijah, is not only logical, but also quite compelling. Perhaps Paul went there for further instruction on his new commission from the Lord, and in the process was shown a revelation of the future catching-up event, as well as the powerful voice of the trumpet which once more will shake both the earth and heavens at the resurrection of the dead in Christ.

An equally important pattern portends for a global earthshaking at the resurrection of the dead in Christ, and serves to corroborate Paul's revelation of the global shaking resulting from the trumpet voice of God. This pattern is evident within the detailed descriptions of the three resurrections to immortal bodies recorded in the New Testament: Jesus Christ, the many saints of Matthew chapter 27, and the two witnesses of Revelation chapter 11.

3

THE EARTHQUAKE
RESURRECTION PATTERN

The previous chapter examined a connection between the events on Mount Sinai and the last trumpet which will sound at the commencement of the three-stage translation of believers: God's trumpet voice shaking both the earth and the heavens. In this chapter, examination of the three detailed accounts of the resurrection of the dead into immortal bodies in the New Testament will reveal another powerful pattern to be applied to the future resurrection of the dead in Christ.

The Resurrection of Jesus Christ and the Many Saints
There is no actual account of the precise moment of the resurrection of Jesus Christ in the Bible. The chapter headings for the beginning of Matthew chapter 28, Mark chapter 16, Luke chapter 24, and John chapter 20 would be more properly titled "The Discovery of the Empty Tomb" instead of the traditional title such as "The Resurrection." What is described in each of those passages is the discovery of the empty tomb by Mary, the

other women, Peter, and John, not the moment of the resurrection.

But Matthew's gospel also includes some very important clues about what happened at the moment of the resurrection of Christ that the other three gospels do not. Interestingly, however, these clues about the moment of his resurrection are included within the detailed description of the moment of his *death*. According to Matthew 27:50-54, after Jesus cried out, the temple curtain was torn from top to bottom, and he gave up his spirit. Both Mark and Luke are in agreement with this, but only Matthew includes a parenthetical statement regarding a mysterious group of many saints:

> . . . The earth shook and the rocks were split apart. And tombs were opened, and the bodies of many saints who had died were raised. (They came out of the tombs after his resurrection and went into the holy city and appeared to many people.) Now when the centurion and those with him who were guarding Jesus saw the earthquake and what took place, they were extremely terrified and said, "Truly this one was God's Son!" (*Mat 27-51-54*)

All three synoptic gospels then describe a centurion who made a proclamation about Jesus being righteous, the Son of God. Matthew was the only gospel writer to insert into the narrative the details of the shaking of the earth that caused the tombs of many saints to open followed by their resurrection from the dead.

John's gospel does not record any earthquake occurring at Jesus' death or shortly after it. It seems that if any of the gospels should have recorded an earthquake at his death, it would have been John, because he was present at the crucifixion. His gospel, however, records no shaking whatsoever at the death of Jesus. He cried out, "It is finished," bowed his head, and died. John then records that the soldiers came and broke the legs of the two men who were crucified with Jesus in order to speed up their deaths. Then they came to Jesus and found he was dead. Were they running away in fear because of the earth shaking and the rocks splitting? No. Instead, one of the Roman guards found time to thrust a spear into the side of the Lord, causing blood and water to flow out. Later, Joseph of Arimathea and Nicodemus came and took Christ's body off the cross after petitioning Pilate for permission to do so. Still no mention of an earthquake in John's gospel.

An Earthquake at His Resurrection

For these reasons, the best explanation for the earthquake of Matthew 27:54 is that it was an earthquake that occurred at the resurrection of Jesus Christ, followed by the many saints. The verse is a summary of the reaction of the centurion and the guards of the entire death and resurrection sequence as encapsulated within Matthew 27:51-53. The main consideration for this conclusion is the opening of the tombs of the many saints. Unless their tombs came open without a shaking of the earth, there had to be an earthquake at the moment of the resurrection of Jesus Christ, not his death. Otherwise, the tombs of the many saints would have been open while their dead bodies remained in place during the entire time Christ was also dead in the tomb, three days and three nights. Matthew's gospel records that the saints came out of their graves only after Christ had been raised from the dead. The best explanation is that they came out of their tombs after the shaking of the earth at Christ's resurrection.

In order for the earthquake and opening of the tombs to have occurred at the moment of Jesus' *death*, the many saints would have been resurrected to immortality *before* him. If they were resurrected before Christ when the earth shaking of Matthew chapter 27 is recorded, then Christ was not the firstfruits of the resurrection of the dead. But Paul made it clear in I Corinthians 15:20-23 that Christ was the firstfruits of the resurrection to an immortal body:

> But now Christ has been raised from the dead, the firstfruits of those who have fallen asleep. (*I Cor 15:20*)

Therefore, there is no other logical interpretation than to state that the resurrection of these saints occurred after the resurrection of Jesus Christ, and thus, the shaking of the earth which also caused their tombs to open must have taken place at the moment of Christ's resurrection.

Were these many saints raised from the dead back into their mortal bodies? Unless there was a mass execution of righteous Jews in Jerusalem three to four days prior to the Passover, this is not possible. Only then would there be enough saints to be called "many" that would be available to be resurrected back into a mortal body. But neither the gospels nor the historical record make reference to such a genocidal slaughter. Therefore, the bodies of these saints would have been decomposed past the point that there could have been a resurrection back into their mortal bodies, such as was possible with the raising of Lazarus and several other resurrections to mortal bodies recorded in the Bible. Therefore, these many saints must have been resurrected into immortal bodies.

If this interpretation is correct, then three things happened just after the moment of the *resurrection* of Christ:

1. An earthquake – a shaking of the earth
2. The tombs in and surrounding the city were opened, and

3. Many bodies of the saints who had died were raised from the dead to immortality, and were seen walking about the streets of Jerusalem.

The Resurrection of the Two Witnesses

The third resurrection of the dead to immortality coinciding with a powerful earthquake is that of the two witnesses of Revelation chapter 11, a resurrection that has yet to take place but is described in detail. The two witnesses are described as two individuals who will appear on the earth in the future to give a testimony and prophesy for 42 months. A great deal of detail about their specific mission is provided in Revelation chapter 11, however, their specific identity is kept hidden. When their time of testimony is completed, they will be killed by the beast from the abyss, and their dead bodies will lie in the streets of Jerusalem for three and a half days. Suddenly, God will resurrect them and seize them into the air in the sight of all. Just as their resurrection takes place, there will be a large earthquake that shakes the city of Jerusalem:

> Just then a major earthquake [*mégas seismós*] took place and a tenth of the city collapsed; seven thousand people were killed in the earthquake, and the rest were terrified and gave glory to the God of heaven. (*Rev 11:13*)

Combining the resurrection to immortality of Jesus, the many saints, and the two witnesses, a common characteristic is the presence of earthquakes immediately after the resurrection. The power released upon the earth when individuals are resurrected to immortality appears to be responsible for the earthquakes that are recorded in each case. In Ephesians chapter 1, Paul referenced the immense energy and power that God displayed in raising Christ from the dead:

and what is the incomparable greatness of his power toward us who believe, as displayed in the exercise [*enérgeia*] of his immense strength. This power he exercised [*energéo*] in Christ when he raised him from the dead and seated him at his right hand in the heavenly realms (*Eph 1:19-20*)

The Shroud of Turin - Image of the Resurrection Power?

There is evidence of that immense energy and supernatural power present at the resurrection of Jesus Christ on what many scientists and researchers believe is his burial linen, a cloth that has been preserved since the resurrection event: the Shroud of Turin. This cloth was procured by Joseph of Arimathea and Nicodemus, in which they wrapped his body according to Jewish burial customs. When Peter arrived at the empty tomb, he observed the cloth lying in the tomb.

It is not the aim of this section to fully describe the Shroud, nor to exhaustively cover all the reasons why it may or may not be the burial cloth of Jesus Christ. Whether the shroud is or is not the actual burial linen of Christ should have no bearing on the Christian faith. For a brief summary of its history and supernatural characteristics that lead to the conclusion that the Shroud of Turin is the burial shroud of Jesus, see chapter six of my previous book, *Earthquake Resurrection*.

What do the experts who have meticulously studied this shroud believe caused the image to form on the cloth in the amazing way that it did? This question will be explored to understand its significance with respect to the future resurrection of the dead in Christ and the transformation of the bodies of believers. Thaddeus Trenn, Director of the Science and Religion Course Programme at the University of Toronto, stated that there was a primary, triggering event that caused the X-ray phenomena that are present on the Shroud of Turin: what he termed an "influx of energy."[1]

Dr. Alan Whanger, professor emeritus of Duke University Medical Center and Director of the Council for the Study of the Shroud of Turin, stated that some scientists have suggested that "a controlled nuclear event" occurred at the moment of the resurrection in which the Lord's body gave off a massive amount of radiation, then "dematerialized and passed through the Shroud, leaving a kind of negative photograph with an X-ray component . . ."[2] It is evident what kind of effect the power of Christ's resurrection had on the shroud, leaving behind an X-ray, three-dimensional photograph at the moment of the incredible event. Is it possible that this same resurrection power to raise Jesus, the many saints, and the two witnesses caused the earthquakes that were associated with each of their resurrections? Consider what Dr. Alan Mills, quoted by noted author and shroud historian Ian Wilson, stated on this possibility:

> Another hypothesis, put forward by Dr. Allan Mills of Leicester University, suggests that the image might have been created by some type of electrical discharge between body and cloth, associated perhaps with the earthquake activity described by the Evangelist Matthew as having occurred while Jesus' corpse lay in the tomb.[3]

Dr. Mills believes that there may be a connection between the electrical discharge that took place at the moment of his resurrection and the earthquake activity described in Matthew's gospel. Dr. Kitty Little, a former nuclear physicist, stated that the image on the shroud could have been caused by an instantaneous nuclear explosion of light and energy, which would account for the well-defined image as well as the earthquake described in the gospels.[4]

These scientists and researchers believe that the earthquake described in the account of the resurrection of Jesus Christ may have been due to the nuclear discharge during the resurrection event. If the resurrection power to raise Jesus Christ, the many saints, and the two witnesses caused the earthquakes that were associated with each of their resurrections, then what does this forecast for the future simultaneous resurrection of the dead in Christ?

Earthquakes at the Resurrection of the Dead in Christ

If the Shroud of Turin is indeed the linen shroud of Jesus Christ, then there is an actual three-dimensional photograph of the moment of Jesus Christ's resurrection to immortality on the shroud. Scientists have used words such as "nuclear event," "instantaneous," and "dematerialized," in describing what happened at the resurrection moment. If this is indeed what happened at the moment of Jesus Christ's resurrection, the implications for believers at the resurrection of the dead in Christ are profound.

Consider the magnitude of an exponentially larger resurrection of the dead in Christ in the future. Untold millions, perhaps billions, of those who have died in covenant with Jesus Christ throughout history will be instantaneously and simultaneously resurrected from the dead and transformed to immortality with the same dynamic power described in the resurrections of Jesus Christ, the many saints, and the two witnesses. With all this supernatural activity happening in a moment's time, might it be possible that severe geologic activity will result, causing a magnetic disturbance and changes to the structure of the earth's surface?

If the magnitude of this energy is unleashed worldwide at the resurrection event, in concert with the sounding of the last trumpet voice of God that will shake the heavens and the earth, a massive worldwide catastrophe would ensue. Worldwide earthquakes, volcanic activity due to displaced magma, tsunamic activity due to the massive earthquakes, perhaps even a shifting of the earth's magnetic poles or worse, the crust itself, the movement of mountains and islands, and more, would result from this powerful instantaneous event.

As alluded to in the previous chapter, the description of the opening of the sixth seal includes a list of events that fit perfectly with such a global shaking occurring at the resurrection of the dead in Christ:

> Then I looked when the Lamb opened the sixth seal, and a huge earthquake took place; the sun became as black as sackcloth made of hair, and the full moon became blood red; and the stars in the sky fell to the earth like a fig tree dropping its unripe figs when shaken by a fierce wind. The sky was split apart like a scroll being rolled up, and every mountain and island was moved from its place. (*Rev 6:12-14*)

Take notice of the huge earthquake and the movement of every mountain and island from its current position on the earth. This is perfectly consistent with significant seismic activity, as well as a magnetic or partial crustal pole shift.

For these reasons, the opening of the sixth seal is a compelling candidate for the moment of the resurrection of the dead in Christ at the sounding of the last trumpet of God's voice, resulting in the shaking of the earth and the heavens as described in Haggai 2:6, Hebrews 12:26, and Revelation 6:12-14. It will occur within the blink of an eye, and it will leave in its wake a catastrophic change to the surface of the earth.

But is there any justification for choosing the events of the sixth seal as a description of the future catastrophic effect of the resurrection of the dead in Christ and transformation of the bodies of believers in immortal bodies? Jesus provided corroboration for a massive destruction at his return by making reference to two catastrophic events of the ancient past, and Paul told the Thessalonian believers that the day of the Lord's wrath would be ushered in by "sudden destruction." A closer inspection of the destructive events described in the sixth seal, as well as the setting of the opening of the five seals before it, will be beneficial to determine whether these passages describe the same event to which both Jesus and Paul made reference: the "sudden destruction" at the future return of Jesus Christ to earth.

---

[1] Trenn, Thaddeus, interviewed by Linda Moulton Howe. "X-File on the Shroud," British Society for the Turin Shroud, Issue, 49, June 1999.
[2] Parker, Shafer. "The Shroud of Turin: Latest Research Bolsters Authenticity," National Catholic Register, 2002.
[3] Wilson, Ian (1986). *The Mysterious Shroud*, p. 126. New York: Doubleday.
[4] Little, Dr. Kitty. "The Application of Scientific Methods to the Turin Shroud," http://www.shroud.com/bsts4607.htm, accessed September 21, 2004.

4

SUDDEN DESTRUCTION OF THE SIXTH SEAL

T he convergence of supernatural events within the natural world, in such a brief amount of time, will cause incredible things to happen to the natural world. In his resurrection body, Jesus was able to move into and out of the normal three-dimensional world of length, width, and height, as well as the fourth dimension continuum of space-time, in which humans are currently constrained. The interference between the natural world and the unseen supernatural world will bring sudden destruction on the earth.

Looking closely at the description of the sixth seal, other than the opening of the seal by the Lamb, there is no cause given for the many effects listed. What follows the opening is a description of things happening on the earth and in the sky. The first four seals all feature some kind of natural effect upon the earth, such as war, disease, and famine. But in each case, the cause is revealed: a white, red, black, and pale green horse with a rider, symbolizing a spirit unleashed on the earth.

The *unmentioned cause* setting in motion the catastrophic sixth seal events, according to this prophetic model, will be the future three-stage resurrection, transformation, and catching-up event, set in motion by the last trumpet voice of God and the power of the global resurrection of the dead in Christ, shaking both the heavens and the earth. The convergence of this supernatural mega-event within the natural world will result in the effects seen in Revelation 6:12-14.

Sudden Destruction: The Days of Noah and Lot
Many may be resistant to the idea that the resurrection and catching-up event will be ushered in by a worldwide catastrophe that would likely cause the deaths of many people. Yet, that is exactly what both Jesus and Paul stated would be the case. According to Paul, the day of the Lord will be introduced with "sudden destruction:"

> For you know quite well that the day of the Lord will come in the same way as a thief in the night. Now when they are saying, "There is peace and security," then sudden [*aiphnídios*] destruction comes on them, like labor pains on a pregnant woman, and they will surely not escape [*ekphúgōsin*]. (*1 The 5:2-3*)

In the natural, a thief in the night comes when the people are sleeping, unaware of the sudden destruction coming on them. In a spiritual sense, those who are not prepared for the coming of the Lord will be caught in an unprepared state, unable to escape what comes upon them. The Greek words used by Paul in explaining the quick destructive power that introduces the day of the Lord are the same used by Jesus when he was explaining the day of the Lord to his disciples:

"But be on your guard so that your hearts are not weighed down with dissipation and drunkenness and the worries of this life, and that day close down upon you suddenly like a trap [*aiphnídios*]. For it will overtake [*pagís*] all who live on the face of the whole earth. But stay alert at all times, praying that you may have strength to escape [*ekphígein*] all these things that must happen, and to stand before the Son of Man." (*Luk 21:34-36*)

Unlike those upon whom the day of the Lord comes like a thief, Jesus stated there will be those who will escape the catastrophic destruction which will introduce the day of the Lord. The same Greek word is used to describe the escape, *ekpheúgō*, which was used by Paul in describing the fate of those who will be caught by surprise by the sudden destruction. In addition, both of the passages use *aiphnídios* to describe the swift and severe manner in which the destruction will come. The Greek *pagís* is a noun which means a trap set for animals resulting in their destruction and capture. This noun was used to describe the fate of all those who are not ready at his coming.

Most popular books and movies about the future catching-up event feature a globe in basically the same physical condition after the event as before it. But, if there is any further doubt about whether the time of the coming of the Lord will be a time of catastrophe on the earth, one need only examine Luke chapter 17, where Jesus himself warned that the time of his revealing would feature destructive events patterned after those in the days of Noah and Lot. Jesus began a discourse to his disciples about the future with a reference to his lightning-flash appearance:

Then people will say to you, 'Look, there he is!' or 'Look, here he is!' Do not go out or chase after them. For just like the lightning flashes and lights

up the sky from one side to the other, so will the
Son of Man be in his day. (*Luk 17:23-24*)

In contrast to those who will be looking for the Lord to first
appear on the earth, Jesus stated there will be an appearance in
which he comes just as quickly as the lightning flashes through
the sky. This description is in agreement with Paul's description
of the resurrection and transformation event taking place in a
moment, in the blinking of an eye, in which Jesus will return in
the sky to catch up all believers who are resurrected and
transformed. Jesus continued the discussion by providing two
dramatic, historic examples of what to expect on the earth at the
time of this lightning-flash appearance:

> Just as it was in the days of Noah, so too it will be
> in the days of the Son of Man. People were
> eating, they were drinking, they were marrying,
> they were being given in marriage—right up to
> the day Noah entered the ark. Then the flood
> came and destroyed them all. (*Luk 17:26-27*)

First, he compared the time of his coming to the days of
Noah. Up until the day Noah entered the ark, the world went on
as usual, and there was no reason for panic. However, on the day
the flood began, the inhabitants of the earth quickly realized
their predicament. The violent changes that took place on the
earth destroyed all of them. The day overtook them as a thief,
and the planet underwent legendary changes which no living
creature outside the ark survived. Jesus stated it would be the
same when he returns in the sky. He next reminded the disciples
of the days of Lot:

> Likewise, just as it was in the days of Lot, people
> were eating, drinking, buying, selling, planting,
> building; but on the day Lot went out from

> Sodom, fire and sulfur rained down from heaven
> and destroyed them all. It will be the same on the
> day the Son of Man is revealed. (*Luk 17:28-30*)

The sudden destruction of Sodom and Gomorrah, as chronicled in Genesis chapter 19, resulted from the cities being pelted with supernatural fire and sulfur from the sky. Jesus then stated it will be "the same" when he returns; some type of destruction will take place on the earth at his lightning-quick revelation.

According to this passage in Luke chapter 17, when Jesus appears in the sky like a lightning flash, the appearance will be followed by natural disasters on the earth similar to the flood of Noah's day and the destruction of Sodom by fire and sulfur from heaven. He clearly stated that the same conditions would be found on the earth when his appearance took place, and went into a fair amount of detail in the description. One should expect, therefore, that when the Son of Man is revealed in the future, and appears like lightning in the sky, the earth will experience similar types of destruction.

Both Noah's family and Lot and his two daughters escaped the destruction of their day, representing a righteous remnant similar to the remnant that will completely escape the destruction that will take place on the earth at the time of the future three-stage event. To suggest that belief in a catching-up event prior to the day of the Lord's wrath is "escapism" is justified, as Jesus himself used the word "escape" to introduce an alternative to going through these destructive events. Earth's surviving inhabitants who do not escape will be trapped in the midst of the devastation.

The Sixth Seal Blood-Red Moon
There are three solid pieces of scriptural corroboration which support the placement of the beginning of the day of the Lord's

wrath after the opening of the sixth seal. Revelation 6:12 includes the first of these corroborations, along with a description of the huge shaking of the earth that occurs after the opening of the sixth seal:

> Then I looked when the Lamb opened the sixth seal, and a huge earthquake [*mégas seismós*] took place . . . (*Rev 6:12(a)*)

The first occurrence after the opening of the seal is the major worldwide earthquake, which will occur at the moment of the resurrection of the dead in Christ and the changing of the bodies of believers into immortal ones. This conclusion is based on (1) the sounding of God's trumpet voice, the last trumpet, once more shaking the heavens and the earth, and (2) the continuation of the pattern of earthquakes accompanying the resurrection to immortality, similar to the resurrection of Jesus, the many saints, and the two witnesses, as described in previous chapters.

The final clause of verse 12 contains the first piece of corroboration that the sixth seal must occur before the day of the Lord's wrath:

> . . . the sun became as black as sackcloth made of hair, and the full moon became blood red; (*Rev 6:12(b)*)

There are several verses in the Old Testament in which the prophets revealed that both the sun and the moon will withdraw their shining, implying that these heavenly bodies will somehow be shaded or covered relative to the earth, which could be accomplished by the presence of large amounts of volcanic ash in the atmosphere. However, there is only one Old Testament passage in which the moon is described as turning to a blood-red color, which is in Joel chapter 2:

The sunlight will be turned to darkness and the moon to the color of blood, before the day of the LORD comes—that great and terrible day! (*Joe 2:31*)

There are only two other passages, both in the New Testament, in which the moon is described as turning to a blood-red color. The first is Acts chapter 2, where Peter includes the verse in quoting a passage from Joel during his Feast of Pentecost explanation of the meaning of the gift of the Holy Spirit. The only other reference to the moon turning blood-red is in Revelation 6:12 within the events of the sixth seal. The prophecy of Joel will be fulfilled, therefore, upon the opening of the sixth seal, not before.

The key *when* Joel said this event would happen: "before the day of the Lord comes—that great and terrible day." Above, the "sudden destruction" that will introduce the day of the Lord was explored. Joel's prophecy reveals that, before the day of the Lord commences, the moon will turn to a blood-red color. This disqualifies the traditional notion that the day of the Lord will begin with the opening of the *first* seal, because the blood-red moon is part of the *sixth* seal events.

If the opening of the seven seals are "judgments" during the day of the Lord's wrath, as most traditional prophetic models hold, then Joel's prophecy of the blood-red moon would be fulfilled *after* the day of the Lord begins, resulting in a contradiction between the passages in Joel and Revelation. But Joel's prophecy clearly states that the blood-red moon occurs *before* the day of the Lord begins. Therefore, the opening of the first *six* seals must also occur before the day of the Lord's wrath, not after.

When volcanic eruptions take place, the explosion of lava and ash into the air can cause not only the sunset to appear red globally, but also the moon. This is a powerful connection to what occurs within the description of the sixth seal. Volcanoes would almost certainly be part of a massive worldwide shaking of the earth, in which all mountains and islands move, due to the disturbance of the underlying magma. In the same passage, the prophet Joel made reference to fire and columns of smoke on the earth that would precede the day of the Lord's wrath:

> I will produce portents both in the sky and on the earth —blood, fire, and columns of smoke. (*Joe 2:30*)

This fire and columns of smoke are almost certainly a reference to the eruption of volcanoes. The gaseous pressure built up underneath the earth would cause an explosion of magma, rock, and ash up through the openings in volcanoes all over the world while the earth is shaking. The gases and dust from these explosions would cause the moon to appear a vivid, blood-red color even without a lunar eclipse. An earthquake resurrection of the dead in Christ at the sixth seal, in which the atmosphere filled with gases and dust from seismic and volcanic activity, would cause these effects. Joel 2:30-31, therefore, fits perfectly within the events of the sixth seal, before the great day of the Lord's wrath is unleashed on the earth.

"The Day of Their Great Wrath Has Come"

The second piece of scriptural corroboration which supports the placement of the beginning of the day of the Lord's wrath after the opening of the sixth seal is found in the reaction of the people remaining on the earth:

> Then the kings of the earth, the very important people, the generals, the rich, the powerful, and everyone, slave and free, hid themselves in the caves and among the rocks of the mountains.

> They said to the mountains and to the rocks, "Fall
> on us and hide us from the face of the one who is
> seated on the throne and from the wrath of the
> Lamb, because the great day of their wrath has
> come, and who is able to withstand it?" (*Rev
> 6:15-17*)

According to those remaining on the earth, the great day of
wrath will arrive with, if not *after*, the events of the sixth seal. It
could not be stated any more clearly than, "the great day of their
wrath *has come*." They are referring to the day of the Lord, an
incredible day of wrath that the prophets of the Old Testament
saw and described over and over in great detail. Their statement
provides further proof that the day of the Lord begins at this
point or just after it, not at the opening of the first seal at the
beginning of Revelation chapter 6.

The explanation offered by some traditional pre-millennial
models to alleviate this problem is to separate a "tribulation
period" into two types of wrath: first, the wrath of the Lamb in
Revelation 6:1-14, and second, the wrath of God in the rest of
the book. However, Revelation 6:16 states that the day of *their*
wrath had come at the conclusion of the events of the sixth seal,
not before. Because of this, the resurrection of the dead in Christ
and catching up of believers must occur after the opening of the
first seal, and before the opening of the sixth seal, because the
day of the Lord's wrath begins after the opening of the sixth
seal.

The pronoun "their" preceding "wrath" in verse 17 is
rendered in some translations with "his" using the Greek *autou*,
referring either to the Lamb or the one seated on the throne in
the previous verse. However, the use of the Greek verb *auton* for
"their" is well supported, and also makes the most grammatical
sense. This is because the previous verse refers to two entities:

the one seated on the throne and the Lamb. Since there are two entities, a plural pronoun is appropriate.

When one reads the first four seals of Revelation chapter 6, it is clear that these are symbolic representations of things taking place on the earth. There are not four horses riding around, at least, ones visible to the human eye, carrying out these activities. Because of this, some scholars have concluded that *all* of the seven seal events are to be interpreted symbolically. However, it clearly makes no logical sense to interpret a literal red horse roaming around with a rider who carries a huge sword. Nor does it make logical sense to interpret a literal black horse roaming around with a rider holding a yoke in his hand. The same can be said for the other two horses and riders. However, there is a shift with the opening of the fifth seal:

> Now [*kai*] when the Lamb opened the fifth seal, I saw under the altar the souls of those who had been violently killed because of the word of God and because of the testimony they had given. (*Rev 6:9*)

The translators of the NET Bible state that the first word of this verse signals this shift: "Here *kaív* has been translated as "now" to indicate the introduction of a new and somewhat different topic after the introduction of the four riders."[1] Therefore, from the fifth seal through the end of the chapter, there is no intellectual harm in a *literal* interpretation of the following in the description of the fifth and sixth seal events:

1. An altar under which martyred souls abide.
2. The cry of the martyrs for the avenging of their blood.
3. The white robe and the word of confirmation and comfort.
4. A massive shaking of the earth at the opening of the sixth seal.

5. Changes in the sun, moon, stars, and the heavenly bodies.
6. The effects of the shaking causing mountains and islands to move.
7. The physical and verbal response to the sixth seal events.

The people certainly react to the events of the sixth seal as if they are literally happening on the earth, and so should the reader of the text. They will hide in the rocks and caves, and cry out for the rocks to fall on them for concealment from the wrath of God and the Lamb. Certain parts of the vision of John are clearly symbolic, and certain parts are clearly literal. Judging from the reaction of the inhabitants of the earth to the events of the sixth seal, what is described within the events of the sixth seal will literally happen.

The Scroll Contains the Trumpet and Bowl Judgments
The third piece of scriptural corroboration which supports the placement of the beginning of the day of the Lord's wrath after the opening of the sixth seal, and not with the opening of the first seal, is found with the opening of the seventh seal. Revelation chapter 8 records the opening of the seventh seal:

> Now when the Lamb opened the seventh seal there was silence in heaven for about half an hour. Then I saw the seven angels who stand before God, and seven trumpets were given to them. (*Rev 8:1-2*)

After a time of silence in heaven for about thirty minutes, seven angels are presented with seven trumpets, which when blown, result in devastating judgment on the earth and its inhabitants. It is important to understand that the events of the trumpet and bowl judgments will not be able to take place without the progression of the opening of all seven seals. The seven bowl judgments can take place only after the seventh trumpet is blown, and the seven trumpet judgments can take place only after the seventh seal is opened.

This is important because there has been a tendency by traditional interpreters of the events of the first six seals of Revelation 6:1-17 to equate them with the events of the trumpets and the bowls, claiming they are a restatement of those judgments on the earth, but from a different perspective. For example, John F. Walvoord, former professor, president, and Chancellor Emeritus of Dallas Theological Seminary, taught that the events of the sixth seal will take place near the *end* of the final three and a half years of what he considered to be Daniel's 70th week as a part of God's judgment:

> Revelation 6-18 deals with the last seven years, or more specifically, the last three-and-a-half years preceding the Second Coming.[2] . . .Though this scene [encompassing the events of the sixth seal] is not the final judgment as recorded in Revelation 16 under the seventh bowl of wrath, it indicates that the entire last three-and-a-half years up to the second coming of Christ will be a period of unprecedented trial and trouble for the world as God deals in direct judgment on the world and all its sin.[3]

Similarly, Bruce M. Metzger, a distinguished New Testament scholar and long-time teacher at Princeton Theological Seminary, stated about the seven seals, "The trumpets more or less repeat the revelation of the seven seals, though they present it more from God's standpoint."[4] This has long been the view of traditional pre-millennial models of prophecy for the opening of the seven seals of the scroll.

The view that the events of the sixth seal somehow parallel the events of the trumpet or bowl judgments, and are included near the end of a 7-year "tribulation period," is simply not possible within the chronological flow of Revelation. A simple comparison of the seal events with the trumpet and bowl judgments will yield this conclusion, because the events are different. But beyond a simple reading, it is clear that the trumpet and bowl judgments are contained within the seven-sealed scroll itself, and therefore, the seventh seal must be opened before those judgments can take place. The seal events are mutually exclusive from the judgments because the scroll contains the awful judgments of the day of the Lord's wrath. For these reasons, the events of the sixth seal cannot be a parallel rendition of any part of the trumpet or bowl judgments.

Before leaving the events of the sixth seal completely, the aftermath of such globe-altering events must be given proper attention. The sudden catastrophic events that ensue with the opening of the sixth seal will be a direct result of the trumpet voice of God and the power of the resurrection of the dead, leading to the seventh seal and ushering in the wrath of God. In the future, *all* of the righteous throughout history will be raised with the same power displayed in raising Jesus Christ from the dead. Imagine the aftermath of such a global, destructive event featuring the simultaneous resurrection and disappearance of millions of people. Could it be that the destruction of this event will be able to mask their disappearance?

---

[1] The NET Bible. Notes on Revelation chapter 6, verse 9, note 38.
[2] Walvoord, John F. (1990). *The Prophecy Knowledge Handbook*, p. 552. Wheaton, Illinois: Scripture Press Publications, Inc.
[3] Ibid, p. 557-8.
[4] Metzger, Bruce M. (1993). *Breaking the Code: Understanding the Book of Revelation*, p. 55. Nashville: Abingdon Press.

5

THE AFTERMATH: GLOBAL DISAPPEARANCE

T he seismic and volcanic activity on the earth has seen a major upswing during the time of the writing of this book. In fact, there has been so much activity that it was very difficult to keep up with it. Several severe earthquakes have taken place in Sumatra, Java, Japan and other spots along the Ring of Fire, and several volcanoes have been rumbling around the globe, with some actual eruptions.

Current Seismic and Volcanic Activity
The most shocking seismic event in recent history took place very recently. The second largest earthquake in recorded history, of 9.3 magnitude,[1] occurred on December 26, 2004 approximately 155 miles off the coast of the Indonesian island of Sumatra in the Indian Ocean, six miles below the surface of the ocean floor. The oceanic fault lines slammed into each other, generating nearly 500 mph tsunami waves hurdling toward the

coastlines of Indonesia, Thailand, India, Sri Lanka, Somalia, and several other surrounding nations. This event resulted in the deaths of well over 200,000, with hundreds of thousands declared "missing" and millions of survivors left struggling to find shelter and provisions. The devastation from this event surpassed that of the 1883 eruption of the volcano Krakatoa, which took the lives of over 36,000, as well as the devastation of 1755 when tsunamis killed an estimated 60,000 in Portugal. Eyewitnesses described walls of water 20-30 feet high driving toward the coastlines on a beautifully clear and sunny day, leaving behind ruin as they slammed into the real estate.

In addition to the large waves, this tsunami event was responsible for other startling side effects around the globe. Consider the following:

1. According to the United States Geological Survey, the island of Sumatra, and several smaller surrounding islands, actually slid nearly 120 feet to the southwest when the India and Burma plates slammed into each other in the Indian Ocean.
2. According to geologist Ken Hudnut, "The earthquake has changed the map." He also stated that the orbit of the earth on its axis may have actually wobbled "due the massive amount of energy exerted and the sudden shift in mass."[2]
3. This earthquake sent shockwaves all over the planet, triggering earthquakes as far away as the Mount Wrangell volcano in south-central Alaska,[3] and registering on seismic monitoring equipment as far away as Oklahoma.[4]
4. Scientists found that there was a polar shift from this earthquake. The "mean North pole" shifted approximately 2.5 centimeters.[5]
5. Scientists also stated that the earthquake sped up the orbit of the earth on its axis, shortening the length of a day by less than three microseconds.[6]

6. The quake shook the entire surface of the earth, and weeks after the event, it was still trembling. So much water was displaced from the Bay of Bengal and the Andaman Sea that the worldwide sea level was raised .004 inches.

7. The planet oscillated like a bell every 17 minutes after the quake, which was easily measured with new technology. In addition, the ground moved 0.4 inches everywhere on the planet's surface, though it wasn't discernible in most places. According to scientist Roger Bilham of the University of Colorado, "no point on Earth remained undisturbed." [7]

8. Since the massive earthquake, the islands of Malaysia and Langkawi have been slowly shifting westward rather than the normal eastward shift.

When the descriptions of the December 26, 2004 earthquake and tsunami waves are compared to the description of the events after the opening of the sixth seal, the similarities are quite alarming. A scientist with the Indian government stated that because of the earthquake, the topography and the coastline of the Andaman and Nicobar islands changed, creating a northwest-southeast tilt. Just as the islands of Sumatra and Malaysia moved in response to this earthquake, and just as the entire planet shifted slightly, so every island and mountain will move when the exponentially greater sixth seal events take place. Just as the earth wobbled slightly on its axis due to this earthquake, the earth will shift on its axis and possibly cause the stars to appear to fall toward the earth's horizon when the sixth seal events take place. Just as the length of a day shortened slightly due to this earthquake, so the days during the day of the Lord's wrath may be shortened as a result of the sixth seal events.

There have been other powerful seismic events in addition to this event. A 7.6 magnitude earthquake in Pakistan-controlled Kashmir in October 2005 claimed over 80,000 lives and injured over 100,000, and a 7.7 magnitude earthquake in Java in July 2006, which generated tsunamis, took hundreds of lives, devastated the coastal areas, and displaced thousands. In disasters such as these, scores of people simply could not be accounted for and were therefore labeled as missing. Those unfortunate enough to be in the locale of the activity were described as being in shock and extreme fear of aftershocks. Chaos and looting was rampant, food and water supplies were contaminated, and electricity was compromised in affected areas.

In addition, ominous seismic and volcanic activity has been taking place underneath Yellowstone National Park in Wyoming that, for the most part, is going unreported in the major media. One of the world's largest supervolcanoes is the Yellowstone caldera, located in a 30 by 45 mile section of the park. Scientists believe that in the past, this massive caldera erupted and covered most of the North American continent with ash. There are over 2,000 small to medium earthquakes underneath Yellowstone every year as a result of its positioning on top of a large magma chamber in one of the globe's most geologically active hot spots. Scientists believe the Yellowstone caldera is overdue for a major explosion, and a full-scale eruption could result in millions of deaths and a global catastrophe. Yellowstone is only one of several supervolcanoes scattered throughout the globe.

These global seismic and volcanic events mirror much of the description of the events of the sixth seal, but to a smaller scale, yet the current activity does not support the notion that the coming of the Lord is any closer than it was hundreds of years ago. Earthquakes have been occurring, and volcanoes erupting, ever since the flood, and they will continue to occur in the future. However, the increased frequency of the activity provides corroboration of Jesus' statement that there would be birth pains before the end, just as contractions increase prior to a natural birth. In addition, it serves as a warning to all that the earth is primed for a disaster of epic proportions when the moment of the ages finally arrives.

Approaching the Catastrophic Sixth Seal

As that moment approaches, the signs inside the earth, on the earth, and in the sky will continue to occur. But when that day finally arrives, the sixth seal of the scroll will be opened by the Lamb in heaven, and the following events will take place:

1. The dead in Christ throughout history will be resurrected, awakened by power of God and the trumpet voice of God shaking the earth and the heavens.
2. The bodies of all believers, both those resurrected dead in Christ, and the living and remaining believers, will be transformed into the likeness of Jesus Christ's immortal body.
3. All believers, in transformed immortal bodies, will be suddenly caught up together into the air to meet Jesus Christ.

Meanwhile, the earth and its inhabitants will not be able to avoid the *effects* that the trumpet voice of God and the power of the resurrection of the dead in Christ will have on the natural world. Those effects will include the following:

1. Massive worldwide earthquakes and movement of the continental and oceanic plates, causing the mountains and islands to move from their current geographic locations.
2. Shifting of oceanic plates, causing massive tsunami waves which will devastate entire coastlines, cities, and island nations.
3. Volcanic activity resulting from the movement of the crust of the earth on top of the underlying magma. This will cause

volcanoes across the globe to spew lava and ash into the air. The moon will turn blood-red, and the sun will be blackened.

4. The convergence of supernatural activity with the natural world may cause a polar shift, where a severe shift in the earth's crust causes the poles to move from their current position. This may cause the stars to appear to be "falling" or moving toward the earth's horizon. There may also be meteors or asteroids that strike the earth's surface in association with these events.

This may be visualized in the following scenario: in the briefest of moments, all the dead in Christ are resurrected, and all believers, both those living at the time and those just resurrected, are transformed into immortal bodies as the piercing sound of a reverberating horn-blowing is heard all around the world. People look up in a state of bewilderment wondering what that strange sound and massive shaking could be. Then, the supernatural and the natural world converge. Suddenly, the earth's crust begins to shift on top of energized magma from pole to pole, triggering worldwide seismic, volcanic, and tsunamic activity. The massive Yellowstone Park caldera begins to explode gases, molten lava, and toxic ash across the North American continent; the San Andreas Fault ruptures, splitting California in two; the New Madrid Fault erupts and the Gulf of Mexico floods the Mississippi River as the continental plates shift upward and downward; earthquakes around the oceanic fault lines cause monstrous tsunami waves to strike the coastlines; similar catastrophic events occur around the globe.

As this activity begins to take place and the crust of the earth begins to react, believers will still be on the earth, yet in newly-transformed bodies. Just before the devastation and destruction begins to take its full effect, they are suddenly and forcibly snatched up off the earth into the atmosphere. As they rise, they look down to see the planet they just left shifting, quaking, and exploding below them. On this day, the population of the earth will fall drastically due to the exit of living believers and the deaths of many millions of people in the sudden destruction of the events of the sixth seal.

Masking a Global Disappearance

The technological infrastructure of the cities of the earth will be at least severely crippled, if not completely destroyed, as a result of this powerful resurrection event. Electric power will be unavailable, making communication between other nations very difficult. Communication by radio waves may be the best form of communication at that time, providing both parties attempting to communicate have functioning equipment and the required electricity to transmit the signal. The areas with the greatest numbers in which the dead in Christ are buried may experience a higher proportionate share of the supernatural power of the resurrection, resulting in more intense destruction.

As for the whereabouts of missing believers on the earth after the events of the sixth seal, perhaps, due to the worldwide calamity and devastation, they will be claimed as missing or dead; casualties of the chaos. Their vanishing may be completely overlooked due to the masking characteristic that the associated destruction will bring. Will there be news reports of people missing, or will the physical, logistical, and technological infrastructure on the earth be so disrupted and damaged as to prevent this? If satellites that enable worldwide television and cellular phone communications are disabled by the supernatural power of the future translation event, then the ability to disseminate news will be severely crippled. At a bare minimum, satellites will likely require repositioning to compensate for the movement of the earth's surface, as well as other natural and supernatural phenomena that may disrupt their proper functioning. In addition, electricity plants may be completely powered down or otherwise damaged by the electromagnetic activity, or by the shifting of the earth's crust and tsunami damage.

If these scenarios prove to be correct, flash newscast reports of millions of people disappearing around the earth, suggested in popular movies, songs, and books, would be impossible. While the news may be slowly spread by word of mouth, confusion and chaos will ultimately rule the day. Perhaps some of the islands and countries that were formerly accessible or inhabitable will be completely covered underwater, or the land so marred by the earthquakes, volcanoes, and tsunamis, that an accounting for the whereabouts of people is simply impossible.

This type of chaos was clearly evident in the aftermath of the December 26, 2004 tsunami event. Entire cities, one with a population over 100,000, were 80-100% destroyed. Several smaller islands off the coast of Sumatra had simply "disappeared."[8] According to some estimates, over 164,000 people were missing, meaning they were not counted among the dead or injured. After a certain amount of time, the missing persons would be considered among the dead. For example, Great Britain announced on January 16, 2005, over two weeks after the event, that the missing would be declared dead if they were not found after one year.[9] On January 19, 2005, when approximately 70,000 Indonesian people who were previously among the missing were declared among the dead, Indonesian President Yudhoyono stated "Perhaps we will never know the exact scale of the human casualties."[10] Indeed, widespread confusion has ruled the day during the entire process of trying to assess the dead. According to one source from Jakarta, Indonesia, "the massive levels of destruction wrought by the tsunami and the sheer numbers of corpses meant that in the early post-disaster stages, many of the victims were buried in mass graves without prior identification."[11]

Imagine the chaos that will occur at the sixth seal when the effects of the Southeast Asia catastrophe are multiplied many times over on a worldwide basis. Many millions could be missing, and as such, those believers who were living and remaining prior to the event, but could not be found afterward, would simply be declared part of a massive group of missing persons, and eventually would be declared dead in the catastrophe. This is a very solid and plausible explanation for the future disappearance of millions of believers on the earth, a question that has perplexed Bible prophecy students for decades.

Unification Among the Chaos

After some time passes, the planet's surviving inhabitants will begin to pick up the pieces. In the wake of past catastrophic events, human nature has always been to pull together and become united for a common cause. This was the case in the wake of what happened to the United States on September 11, 2001. Citizens banded together when media broadcast showed the planes hitting the buildings and the towers coming down. When such a natural disaster occurs on the earth in the future, affecting each and every nation, a spirit of unity will manifest itself to come together for a common cause, and to rise from the ashes to rebuild.

The response of other nations around the world after the December 26, 2004 earthquake and tsunami in the Indian Ocean provides more evidence of unification of people to regroup and rebuild. Consider the initial response of these nations to help the affected region after this terrible disaster:

- United Nations Secretary General Kofi Annan announced the UN would send disaster and coordination teams to the region for relief and rescue assistance.

- The Russian government sent a helicopter, tents, and equipment to help the relief effort.
- The Chinese government promised to provide emergency humanitarian aid.
- The Canadian government pledged approximately $800,000 in relief aid, as well as other humanitarian assistance on the ground.
- The Philippine government promised a group of humanitarians to help with rescue and cleanup.
- The Australian government sent two Air Force crafts full of medical supplies and blankets, and pledged $7,000,000.
- The United States government pledged an initial $15,000,000 relief package, then later an additional $20,000,000, and stood ready to help in other ways.
- The French government sent a plane of 100 doctors to Sri Lanka.
- The European Union offered approximately $4,000,000 immediately and said more would be offered in the future.
- The Israeli government promised to send doctors and experts.
- The Pakistani government launched a humanitarian search and rescue mission, mobilized its Navy to help the search, and dropped emergency food supplies.
- Greece sent a plane with 11 tons of medical supplies.
- The governments of Germany, Ireland, Britain, and Kuwait all promised monetary assistance.
- The government of Singapore sent a special emergency consular team to Thailand. [12]

The unification that resulted from this disaster was unprecedented, and is a preview of what will likely occur after the sixth seal events have taken their toll. While every nation on the planet will be affected by the events, the nations will come together to help each other.

On the coattails of this unification, perhaps the Middle East peace situation, at an impasse for so long, will finally be settled when a man is able to draw the Palestinians and Jews together over the division of Israel's covenant land. In light of this possibility, consider comments by former United States President Bill Clinton in connection with the devastating December 26, 2004 earthquake and tsunami:

> I am grateful for the opportunity that this terrible tragedy gives for religious reconciliation in the world. . .[in which people around the world are] "reaching out for the Muslims of Indonesia, for the Hindus and the Buddhists, and the Muslims and the Christians in Sri Lanka to reconcile.[13]

Imagine a worldwide catastrophe affecting all ethnic and religious groups, and the chance for reconciliation. Could not the Jews and the Palestinians also fit in that list if a similar catastrophe thrust them into reconciliation mode? Tensions between the Hindus and Buddhists were very high prior to the event, but after the event, there was a temporary lull in the fighting and hatred. Below is a list of specific examples of peace between bitter enemies not only after the 2004 tsunami disaster, but also after other natural disasters in history:

1. After the December 26, 2004 earthquake and resulting tsunami, Pakistan, a bitter nuclear enemy of India, sent relief teams to India and dispatched their Navy to help with the rescue effort. Conflicts between the Muslim population of Pakistan and the Hindu population of India were temporarily set aside due to the disaster.

2. Another temporary reconciliation after the 2004 earthquake and tsunami included a separatist group in Banda Aceh, Indonesia, who announced a unilateral cease-fire in order to help people who were affected by the tragedy. According to Sidney Jones, the Southeast Asia project director for the International Crisis Group, "This is a watershed. . .the tsunami will change the dynamic of the conflict in a number of important ways."

3. Again after the 2004 earthquake and tsunami, the Tamil Tigers were quelled in their resistance against the Sri Lanka central government. According to Hans Brattskar, the Norwegian ambassador to Sri Lanka, "This was definitely one of those events that change history. We are in darkness now, but people are looking for rays of hope."

4. In 2003, the United States provided 68 tons of relief to Bam, Iran after an earthquake devastated the city and killed over 31,000 people. The United States and Iran were not friendly countries prior to the earthquake, but the United States set aside differences in the face of a humanitarian emergency.

5. In 1999, both Greece and Turkey were rocked by severe earthquakes. Tensions were quelled amongst the bitter enemies when rescue crews were sent from both countries to help each other. According to Soli Ozel, teacher of politics at Bilgi University in Istanbul, Turkey, "Suddenly, the perception of the 'other' as evil changed. The earthquakes provided indispensable public support for the policy of rapprochement." [14]

Humanity has consistently responded in a spirit of unity to help in the time of natural disasters, and the events of the sixth seal will certainly be no different. The world will be drawn together in a massive effort to rebuild what has been toppled, and to salvage what is salvageable.

Many will not survive the events of the sixth seal, but those who do will not find much solace. They will be thrust into a period about which Jesus said no one would survive unless its time span were shortened: the days of God's vengeance on the earth. According to Paul in II Thessalonians, it will be a time of great delusion due to the emergence of the prophesied man of sin, who will deceive the surviving humanity. God will send a strong deluding influence on those who survive the destruction of the sixth seal and the trumpet judgments, so that they will believe what is false and be condemned.

It will also be a time of great death and horror due to the destructive events within the trumpet and bowl judgments that will come upon the earth. Jesus prophesied unparalleled suffering during the pouring out of God's vengeance:

> For then there will be great suffering unlike anything that has happened from the beginning of the world until now, or ever will happen. (*Mat 24:21*)

This concludes the first section. Within it, we have examined Paul's mysterious journey to Mount Sinai in Arabia; its connection with the last trumpet voice of God before the resurrection of the dead and the catching up of believers; the pattern of earthquakes coinciding with the resurrection of the dead to immortality; the sudden destruction at the opening of the sixth seal and its connection with the beginning of the day of the Lord's wrath; and aftermath models from historic disastrous events which may prove to be predictive of the aftermath of the sixth seal events. With the foundation of this catastrophic sixth seal resurrection model established, Revelation chapters 4 through 7 will now be examined to understand how this model fits within the chronology of these most important chapters of Bible prophecy. Be prepared for an interesting journey from the first century ascension of Jesus Christ to the future seventh seal ceremony of incense that precedes the unleashing of the wrath of God.

[1] News@nature.com. "Sea Bed Reveals Earthquake Scars," accessed February 12, 2005.

[2] Channelnewsasia.com. "Deadly Quake Rattled Earth Orbit, Changed Map of Asia: Geophysicists," accessed December 28, 2004.

[3] Newkerala.com. "Periodic Tremors at volcano Mt. Wrangell in Arctic Region," accessed February 12, 2005.

[4] Oklahoma Geological Survey. "Earthquake Press Release 9:00pm CST Dec 26, Sunday," accessed February 12, 2005 on ogs.ou.edu.

[5] Physorg.com. "Earthquake Affects Earth's Rotation," accessed January 15, 2005.

[6] Newsday.com. "Did Quake Trim Day Length?," accessed December 28, 2004.

[7] CBS 2 – New York News. "Tsunami Quake Shook Entire Earth," accessed May 21, 2005 on wcbstv.com.

[8] Bernama.com. "Indonesia Needs Help, Death Toll Expected to Exceed 400,000," accessed December 31, 2004.

[9] News.telegraph. "Tsunami Missing to be Declared Dead after a Year," accessed January 15, 2005 on telegraph.co.uk.

[10] Yahoo News. "Global Tsunami Death Toll Tops 226,000," accessed January 20, 2005 on news.yahoo.com.

[11] Yahoo News. "Indonesia Drastically Reduces Possible Tsunami Death Toll," accessed April 10, 2005 on news.yahoo.com.

[12] China View. "International Community Rushes Aid to the Tsunami-hit Countries," accessed December 27, 2004 on xinhuanet.com.

[13] Yahoo News Asia. "Tsunami Tragedy to Boost Religious Unity, Reduce Terrorism: Clinton," accessed January 15, 2005 on asia.news.yahoo.com.

[14] The Christian Science Monitor. "From Sparta to Nicaragua, Disasters Alter Political History," accessed January 15, 2005 on csmonitor.com.

SECTION II

THE REVELATION: FROM ASCENSION TO RESURRECTION

6

ASCENSION TO THE RIGHT HAND OF GOD

I n the supernatural act of ascending to heaven, Jesus Christ passed from one dimensional realm, the physical, earthly realm, into another dimensional realm, the unseen, heavenly realm. Everyone is familiar with the fact that his ascension is described in the New Testament from the earthly perspective, when Jesus took the disciples to the Mount of Olives and was taken up into the clouds and eventually out of their sight. The disciples were promised that he would in the future return to the earth in the same way they saw him ascend, confirming his promise in John chapter 14 that he would come a second time. But is there the same awareness of the New Testament description of his ascension from the *heavenly* perspective? This description is recorded in Revelation chapters 4 and 5, when the Lamb that had been slain appeared in the throne room and took his place at God's right hand.

They Came Preaching About a Kingdom

When the Lord brought the children of Israel out of Egypt and led them to Mount Sinai, he proclaimed that he wanted a kingdom: a kingdom of priests with him as their supreme authority. Later in history, when the Israelites desired a physical leader to be their king like the other nations, the Lord allowed a kingdom to be raised up through David. But while this kingdom came partially through the physical world, it would also have a spiritual component. The Lord told David in II Samuel chapter 7 that, when he died, he would establish a permanent dynasty through his offspring.

The Jewish people therefore knew that they were to look for a descendant of David to be their king, who would establish a permanent dynasty in Israel. The prophet Daniel was shown symbolic visions of the kingdom of God in Daniel chapters 2 and 7, a kingdom that would bring about the demise of the other earthly kingdoms and never be destroyed. Daniel was further shown by the angel Gabriel the coming of the Anointed One, a prince or leader. Therefore, when John the Baptist and Jesus came hundreds of years later declaring that the kingdom of God was near, the people rightly questioned whether either of them were "the Christ," or the Anointed One, the prophesied son of David who would establish the long-awaited kingdom of God on the earth. When they heard Jesus' words and saw his miracles, they were sure he was the son of David and once even tried to make him a king by force.

It was at this point that Jesus introduced the spiritual side to the kingdom of God. When the Pharisees asked when the kingdom of God was coming in Luke chapter 17, Jesus told them the kingdom of God was in their midst, though it was not to be observed with signs or a physical location. When questioned by Pilate about whether he was a king, Jesus told him that his kingdom was not of this physical world. It is clear that they did not understand the spiritual side of the kingdom. John the Baptist himself, who declared in the wilderness of Judea that the kingdom of God was near, when thrown into prison, questioned Jesus about whether he was truly the one for whom they were waiting. Even Jesus' closest companions, the apostles, didn't understand the spiritual kingdom Jesus was introducing. After his resurrection, they asked Jesus if he was at that time going to restore the physical kingdom in Israel as their king.

The case could be easily made that the kingdom of God was the most important and frequently-taught concept by Jesus and the New Testament writers. The chronological history that envelops the New Testament begins with John the Baptist in Matthew chapter 3 in Judea, preaching repentance due to nearness of the kingdom of heaven. When John was imprisoned, the first chapter of Mark records that Jesus began to preach the same message in Galilee. New Testament history ends in Acts chapter 28 with Paul preaching the kingdom of God in Rome for two years:

> Preaching the kingdom of God, and teaching those things which concern the Lord Jesus Christ, with all confidence, no man forbidding him. (*Act 28:31*)

In between the beginning and the end of the New Testament chronological history, the kingdom of God was prominent in Jesus' preaching and the epistles of the New Testament. On numerous occasions, Jesus spoke of the kingdom of God in parables, comparing it with natural phenomena. When he commissioned the 70 disciples, he instructed them to tell the people in each town that the kingdom of God had come upon them, whether the town accepted or rejected them. Even after his resurrection, Jesus continued to instruct the apostles about the same topic, speaking to them over a 40-day period "about matters concerning the kingdom of God" (Acts 1:3). These 40 days concluded with Jesus' ascension to heaven. Mark's gospel makes clear the first act Jesus took after his ascension:

> After the Lord Jesus had spoken to them, he was taken up into heaven and sat down at the right hand of God. (*Mar 16:19*)

This is the defining moment of the kingdom of God: Jesus taking his rightful place at the right hand of God. Through his death and resurrection, Jesus was proclaimed the conquering King of Kings and was seated on the throne in heaven with his Father. It is essential to understand the kingdom of God, and Jesus' ascension to God's right hand, in order to grasp the vision that John was shown in Revelation chapters 4 and 5: the entrance of Jesus Christ to take his place at the right hand of God.

The kingdom of God was the focus of Jesus' teaching, and the writers of the New Testament confirmed his position of authority in the kingdom of God. Jesus took that position of authority after his ascension to heaven. Is it any surprise that John would be shown a vision of this most important and exquisite event, the ascension of Jesus Christ to his position as King of Kings, from a heavenly perspective?

The Right Hand of God

The throne room scene of Revelation chapters 4 and 5 is majestic and inspiring. John described a throne and the one who was seated on it, as well as four mysterious, six-winged living creatures around it. Also before the throne was a group of 24 figures described as "elders." As Revelation chapter 5 opens, a scroll with seven seals was introduced, which was located in the right hand of God:

Then I saw in *the right hand* of the one who was
seated on the throne a scroll written on the front
and back and sealed with seven seals. (*Rev 5:1*)

The right hand of God was, of course, the prophesied
destination and position of authority of the Lord Jesus Christ.
While there are numerous verses in the Old Testament which
mention God's right hand, there is but one in which the Lord is
prophesied to sit at the right hand of God. Psalm 110:1 is an
important prophecy used by the apostles after the resurrection
and ascension of Christ to prove that Jesus Christ ascended to
heaven as the Lord and Messiah, as well as to prove that he is
superior to angels and equal with God the Father:

Here is the Lord's proclamation to my lord: "Sit
down at my *right hand* until I make your enemies
your footstool!" (*Psa 110:1*)

Jesus placement at the right hand of God is confirmed in
numerous passages throughout the New Testament. As Stephen
was being stoned to death in Acts chapter 7, he actually saw
Jesus standing at God's right hand, ready to welcome him after
his death. In several of their letters, both Paul and Peter proclaim
that Jesus Christ is currently at the right hand of God,
interceding for prayers, including:

Who is the one who will condemn? Christ is the
one who died (and more than that, he was raised),
who is at the right hand of God, and who also is
interceding for us. (*Rom 8:34*)

who went into heaven and is at the right hand of
God with angels and authorities and powers
subject to him. (*I Pet 3:22*)

According to these verses, Jesus should be at God's right hand where the seven-sealed scroll is located. In Hebrews 10:12-13, Paul further revealed that Jesus sat down at God's right hand and would *remain* there until his enemies are made his footstool.

The Lamb Ascends to the Throne

After the scroll is described in God's right hand, a search began for someone to open the scroll. No one, however, was found to open the scroll. This makes a futuristic interpretation of Revelation chapters 4 and 5 problematic at best and impossible at worst. Why? Because if Jesus Christ had already ascended to the throne and been in heaven for nearly 2,000 years when John was given this vision, he should be already seated at the right hand of God, ready to take the scroll. Why would the angel have to call throughout heaven and earth to find him?

The answer is that the scene at the opening of Revelation chapter 5 is not a vision of a future event. In the vision that John was being shown, Jesus had not yet arrived at the throne from the earth. Rather than a description of the throne room scene *after* the future three-stage resurrection, transformation, and catching-up event, Revelation chapters 4 and 5 provide John's vision of the scene at God's throne just prior to, and after, the ascension of Jesus Christ to take his seat at the right hand of God in the first century.

Heaven was searching for someone to take the scroll, and John was weeping because of it. Suddenly, one of the 24 elders proclaimed that the Lion of the tribe of Judah, a descendant of David, had conquered and would be able to open the scroll. Then John saw his entrance:

> Then I saw standing in the middle of the throne
> and of the four living creatures, and in the middle
> of the elders, a Lamb that appeared to have been
> killed. He had seven horns and seven eyes, which

are the seven spirits of God sent out into all the earth. *(Rev 5:6)*

In dramatic fashion, rather than a Lion, a Lamb who had been brutally slain appeared in the middle of the throne room, and was declared worthy to open the seven-sealed scroll. The first action taken by the Lamb after his appearance in the heavenly throne room is critically important. He proceeded to the right hand of the throne of God and took the scroll out the right hand of God:

> Then he [the Lamb] came and took the scroll
> from the right hand of the one who was seated on
> the throne, *(Rev 5:7)*

John was shown the victorious King appearing in heaven after his ascension, then proceeding to the right hand of God, just as described in Mark 16:19! For the first time in the New Testament record, important details are provided about Jesus' first act after his ascension. He took a scroll out of God's right hand, which would contain the earth's future until his return, and began to break its seals.

The Reaction of Heaven to the Ascension

What reaction should be expected when the King ascends to the throne after conquering death and the grave? Without question, there should be rejoicing and adoration of the King, declaring him to be worthy of all praise and honor. This is exactly what the four living creatures and 24 elders, and eventually all the angels of heaven, do when the Lamb appears in the throne room.

Who were these 24 elders, or *presbúteros* in Greek, and what do they represent? *Presbúteros* is used in the New Testament and the Septuagint Old Testament, in every case, in reference to a human being on the earth. The traditional pre-millennial interpretation is that these 24 elders represent human beings in a resurrected state, and therefore the future resurrection and catching up must have already taken place by this point in the Revelation chronology under that interpretation. However, in the case of the Revelation *presbúteros*, they are in heaven seated around the throne of God, and thus are not representative of human beings. In *Earthquake Resurrection*, the 24 elders are identified as a heavenly angelic representation of the Levitical priesthood, serving the high priest Jesus Christ in the eternal Melchizedekan priesthood in the heavenly temple.[1]

There are three important clues within the description of the reaction of the 24 elders and the four living creatures which shed light upon whether these entities are human beings, as well as when the events of Revelation chapters 4 and 5 take place. The first clue is that the 24 elders were holding golden bowls, full of incense. This incense is further described as being the prayers of the saints. The 24 elders, if they are a symbolic representative of human saints in heaven, would not be holding golden bowls which contain their own prayers, as if their prayers would still need to be answered at that point.

However, if the 24 elders represent an angelic order of priests, it would make perfect sense for them to be holding the golden bowls with the prayers of the saints. As these prayers reach the throne, they are offered up as incense before the throne, where the high priest Jesus Christ intercedes before the Father for the saints based on their prayers. The 24 elders were holding golden bowls before the throne in preparation for their offering of the incense upon the altar.

The second clue is found within the song that is sung by the 24 elders and the four living creatures. The key to eliminating the possibility that they are human beings or representative of human beings is the content of the song. There is an important difference between the KJV, which is dependent on the Textus

Receptus, and the NET, as well as several other translations, which are dependent on more numerous and earlier sources:

> They were singing a new song: "You are worthy to take the scroll and to open its seals because you were killed, and at the cost of your own blood you have purchased for God persons from every tribe, language, people, and nation. You have appointed them [*autous*] as a kingdom and priests to serve our God, and they will reign on the earth." (*Rev 5:9-10*)

Compare this rendition to the KJV:

> And they sung a new song, saying, Thou art worthy to take the book, and to open the seals thereof: for thou wast slain, and hast redeemed us to God by thy blood out of every kindred, and tongue, and people, and nation; And hast made us unto our God kings and priests: and we shall reign on the earth. (*Rev 5:9-10 KVJ*)

The passage above in the KJV is a major reason for the traditional interpretation that the 24 elders are representative of human believers in heaven. The KJV uses the pronouns "us" and "we," while the NET and the vast majority of other translations use "them" and "they," including the NIV, NASB and ASV. According to the translation notes supplied with the NET, "The vast majority of witnesses have *aujtouv*" (*autous*, "them") here, while the Textus Receptus reads *hJma*'" (*hēmas*, "us") with insignificant support . . .*There is no question that the original text read aujtouv" here.*"[2] [Emphasis in original]

The NET translators state unequivocally that the original manuscript contained *autous*, the Greek pronoun "them." Furthermore, Revelation 5:8 states that the 24 elders and the four living creatures are worshipping the Lamb, and verse 9 states *they* are singing the song to the Lamb. If the KJV rendition of "us" and "we" is correct, then the four living creatures also claimed to be members of the redeemed, purchased by the blood of Jesus Christ. In addition, they claimed to be part of the kingdom of priests that will reign on earth. It is quite clear that the four living creatures are not human beings: on this point, there is 100% agreement among scholars. Therefore, it makes no logical sense for the four living creatures to be singing this song, using the pronouns "us" and "we." Angelic beings were not redeemed by the blood of Jesus Christ, but they rejoice in heaven when a person is redeemed, and according to I Peter 1:12, they greatly desire to know about the gospel of salvation.

This means that the 24 elders and the four living creatures were not singing about themselves, as rendered by the KJV, but about the redeemed that the Lamb had purchased with his own blood. It is powerful evidence against the interpretation that the 24 elders are human beings or representatives of them, as well as proof that Revelation chapter 5 provides a description of the appearance of the Lamb at his ascension to the heavenly throne room for the first time after his violent death and victorious resurrection.

A New Song?

The description of the song of the four living creatures and 24 elders is the third clue to identifying when the scene in Revelation chapter 5 took place. In verse 9, this song is described as a "new song." If this song, in John's vision, were being sung 2,000 or more years after Jesus' death and resurrection, then why would it be described as "new?" The content of the song would denote something had just happened such that it would deserve that label. But the content of their song, the redemption of Jesus Christ on the cross and his purchase of the saints, took place at a certain time in the past.

The song would not be called "new" unless the actions of the Lamb, as described in the song, had just taken place. Under the traditional pre-millennial view, this song will be sung in the future as believers are gathered around the throne in heaven. But if the redemption of mankind and the establishment of the royal priesthood took place nearly 2,000 years ago and Jesus ascended 40 days after his resurrection, why would they wait so long to sing a "new" song?

The royal priesthood was established when Jesus Christ ratified the new covenant by shedding his blood once and for all. If the new song is sung at least 2,000 years after the establishment of the new covenant, then that would make the establishment of the kingdom of priests referred to in the song a "new" event. But this cannot be the case. In I Peter 2:9, Peter declared that believers *are* a royal priesthood, and John declared in Revelation 1:6 that believers *are* a kingdom of priests, both of which were written in the first century.

The proper interpretation of this new song, therefore, is that it was sung in celebration of the new covenant that had been established at the death and resurrection of Christ nearly 2,000 years ago, not in the future. The content of the song was that Jesus had purchased mankind with his blood and made believers a kingdom of priests, all of which occurred in approximately 31-32 AD. This provides more proof that what John saw in the vision of Revelation chapters 4 and 5 was:

1. The throne room scene just before Jesus' ascension to the throne,
2. The appearance of Jesus in the throne room after his ascension,
3. His procession to the right hand of God to take the seven-sealed scroll, and
4. The reaction of the 24 elders and the four living creatures to his appearance at that particular time.

It is important to remember that John was not seeing the actual events as they took place, but that he was shown a vision of the events which took place at the time of Jesus' ascension. In the chapters to follow, the opening of the first five seals of the scroll at God's right hand will begin to reveal what John was shown would happen in the future from his perspective. The events that take place from the opening of the first seal *until* the future resurrection, transformation, and catching-up event unfold in Revelation chapter 6.

---

[1] See *Earthquake Resurrection: Supernatural Catalyst for the Coming Global Catastrophe*, pp. 161-167, which presents a detailed explanation of the 24 orders of the Levitical priesthood established by David according to the pattern given to Aaron by the Lord on Mount Sinai.
[2] The NET Bible. Notes on Revelation chapter 5, verse 10, note 31.

7

FIRST SEAL: THE SPIRIT OF ANTICHRIST

A s Revelation chapter 6 opens, the Lamb is described as opening the first seal of the scroll that he just took out of the right hand of the Father at the end of Revelation chapter 5. Thousands of years did not pass between his sitting down at the right hand of God and taking the scroll in Revelation chapter 5, and opening the first seal at the beginning of chapter 6. What is described in Revelation chapter 4 through the beginning of chapter 6 should be treated as one continuous vision of the heavenly throne room just prior to, and just after, the first century ascension of Jesus to the right hand of God.

The Four Horses and Riders Represent Spirits

The opening of the seals represented the unlocking and progression of future events from John's first century perspective. The events symbolized within the seals were future and prophetic as he saw them in the first century. One should not assume that the events are only future and prophetic from a *modern-day* perspective. As John saw them unfolding in his vision, they would have been future events, or "what will happen after," from *his* perspective.

The colored horses in Zechariah chapters 1 and 6 may be related to the horses of the four seals. There are several interesting things of which to take note in Zechariah's description of the horses:

> I was attentive that night and saw a man seated on a red horse that stood among some myrtle trees in the ravine. Behind him were red, sorrel, and white horses. Then I asked one nearby, "What are these, sir?" The angelic messenger who replied to me said, "I will show you what these are." Then the man standing among the myrtle trees spoke up and said, "These are the ones whom the LORD has sent to walk about on the earth." (*Zec 1:8-10*)

> The messenger replied, "These are *the four spirits of heaven* that have been presenting themselves before the Lord of all the earth. All these strong ones are scattering; they have sought permission to go and walk about over the earth." The Lord had said, "Go! Walk about over the earth!" So they are doing so. (*Zec. 6:5, 7*)

First, the horses were symbols of spirits that roam the earth, presenting themselves before the Lord. Second, there were four spirits, which could be synonymous with the four riders of Revelation chapter 6. Third, these spirits were presenting themselves before the Lord and seeking permission to walk about in the earth. This is similar language to the angelic "sons of God" and Satan who presented themselves before the Lord and were walking in and through the earth, as described in Job chapters 1 and 2. For example, the passage in Job chapter 2 states:

> Again the day came when the sons of God came to present themselves before the LORD, and Satan also arrived among them to present himself before the LORD. And the LORD said to Satan, "Where do you come from?" Satan answered the LORD, "From roving about on the earth, and from walking back and forth across it." (*Job 2:1-2*)

Answering for the group, Satan revealed that they were roving the earth, just as the spiritual entities in Zechariah chapters 1 and 6. The passages from Job and Zechariah viewed together shed some light on the identity of the four spirits of Zechariah, symbolized by horses in his vision. These four horses symbolize spirits which are given permission by the Lord to carry out various judgments on the earth.

But they also provide a framework for understanding the four horses and riders of the first four seals of John's vision in Revelation chapter 6. These horses should be viewed as spiritual entities that are sent from the Lord to accomplish his will on the earth. Note that the spiritual entities identified in Zechariah chapter 6 requested permission to "scatter" all about the face of the earth, and the spiritual entities in Job chapters 1 and 2 requested permission to oppress Job. In each case, the Lord granted permission for them to do so. Applying this to the four horses and riders of Revelation chapter 6, they should be understood in the same way: as messengers sent from before the Lord, accomplishing what he allowed them to accomplish. In the vision of the opening of the first four seals, John was allowed to see the spiritual view of how and why events were going to take

91

place on the earth. Spiritual entities were to be unleashed and allowed to wreak havoc beginning in the first century, and the results are described in the narrative of John's vision.

The Symbolism of the First Seal

The opening of the first seal brings forth the symbols of a white horse with an infamous rider:

> I looked on when the Lamb opened one of the seven seals, and I heard one of the four living creatures saying with a thunderous voice, "Come!" So I looked, and here came a white horse! The one who rode it had a bow, and he was given a crown, and as a conqueror [nikōn] he rode out to conquer [nikēsēi]. (Rev 6:1-2)

Within the New Testament, the color white is always used in either a positive or neutral manner. Leukós in Greek, within Revelation alone, is used in many descriptions, including the hair on Jesus' head, various pieces of heavenly clothing, heavenly horses, and God's throne. Given all these positive associations with white, it might seem to make sense that this white horse symbolizes something positive going forth into the earth. Some interpret the opening of the first seal with the symbolism of the white horse and rider as the pouring out the Holy Spirit on the Day of Pentecost as described in Acts chapter 2 and subsequent progression of the kingdom of heaven on earth through the church. Justification for this view is seen in that just as this first horse and rider are given a crown and go forth with a mission to conquer, so Jesus said that the Holy Spirit would reprove the world of sin, righteousness, and judgment, and that the kingdom of God is taken by force. In addition, several references in I John are made to the Christian overcoming the world through faith (2:13-14; 4:4; 5:4-5), and Jesus told the churches of Asia in Revelation chapters 2 and 3 that they could overcome, all using the same Greek word *nikōn* as used in the description of the conquering spirit of the first seal. This view has some merit, in my view, because 10 days after the ascension of Jesus to the right hand of God (Revelation chapters 4-5), the Holy Spirit was poured out on the Day of Pentecost, just as Jesus promised. If the opening of the first seal in Revelation 6:2, then, represents the pouring out of the Spirit and the progression of the kingdom of God through the church as birthed in Acts chapter 2, then it is also in perfect chronological order with the first century ascension to the right hand of God as described in Revelation 5:7.

However, the symbolism of the white horse and rider should be interpreted in a negative rather than a positive manner for several reasons. First and foremost, the other three horses and riders all represent negative events on the earth. To interpret this seal as a positive conquering of the world would be inconsistent within the context of the other three horses and riders. Second, the red horse rider and the pale green horse rider are both granted permission or given their authority to wreak havoc. Similarly, the white horse rider was "given" a crown, a symbol of earthly conquering authority. As with the horses in the passage from Zechariah, to be "given" or "granted" authority means that the Lord gave them permission to carry out their acts. God would not need to grant himself permission to pour out the gift of the Holy Spirit.

Third, Jesus prophesied in Matthew 24:5 that his name would be used for false pretenses after he was gone and before the end of the age. He prophesied that many would come saying, 'I am the Christ,' and deceive many people. Thus, a white horse symbolizing the *use* of Christ's name to conquer the people under false pretenses is an interpretation supported by Jesus' own predictions. Fourth, Jesus did not advocate the use of force or a conquering spirit when he instructed the disciples to preach the gospel. To repent and trust Christ is a decision that all men must make free of a conquering spirit. In contrast, the white horse rider is bent on being a *nikōn* in Greek, or conqueror. While the Holy Spirit reproves the world of sin and the kingdom of God has overcome the kingdom of darkness, this is a battle won within the conscience of each individual.

Interpreting the Symbolism: Spirit of Religious Domination
For these reasons, the best interpretation of this first seal horse and rider is a symbolism of the spirit of antichrist: a conquering spirit going forth into the earth using a religious system and the name of Christ (a white horse) with conquest and domination of the masses as the goal. The symbols of the bow and crown are further representations of a spirit of conquering and domination. The rider of the white horse should not be interpreted as an actual human being, such as the future Antichrist, any more than the riders of the second, third, and fourth horses should be interpreted as actual human beings. Both the horses *and* their riders are symbolic of a spiritual presence sent forth to ensure an oppressive agenda is carried out in the earth.

In the epistles of the New Testament, the apostles had to defend true Christianity against an evil spirit that had already crept into the churches: the spirit of antichrist. In John's first epistle, he declared that an antichrist was coming in the future, but that *the spirit* of antichrist was already in the world:

> but every spirit that does not confess Jesus is not from God, and this is the spirit of the antichrist, which you have heard is coming, and now is already in the world. (*I Joh 4:3*)

In his second epistle, John declared that deceivers had gone into the world, who denied that Jesus Christ had come in the flesh. These persons were influenced by the spirit of antichrist:

For many deceivers have gone out into the world,
people who do not confess Jesus as Christ coming
in the flesh. This person is the deceiver and the
antichrist! (*II Joh 1:7*)

John was defending true Christianity against Gnosticism, a
heresy birthed from the philosophies of Greek teachers such as
Plato, Socrates, and Aristotle. Gnosticism had already begun to
attach itself to Christianity in the first century. Gnostics believe
that all matter in the physical world is evil and all things spiritual
are good, and that revelation of secret knowledge is granted to a
privileged few served by others who lack the intuitive
wherewithal to receive the revelation.

Early gnostic thought that attached itself to Christianity
embraced Docetism, which is derived from the Greek *dokéō*, or
"to seem." Under Docetism, Jesus Christ's physical body was
only an illusion, as was his crucifixion and resurrection. Greek
philosophy taught against the resurrection of the physical body
because they believed that once a person's evil body dies, their
good spirit was able to freely roam the universe. Paul found this
influence at the church in Corinth:

Now if Christ is being preached as raised from
the dead, how can some of you say there is no
resurrection of the dead? But if there is no
resurrection of the dead, then not even Christ has
been raised. (*I Cor 15:12-13*)

Gnosticism eventually birthed many other heretical teachings
in the first few centuries after Christ's ascension, including
Marcionism, Montanism, and Manichaeism. After the wholesale
persecution of Christianity in the Roman Empire began to die
down after Decius, and later after Diocletian and the ascent of
Constantine, many ante-Nicene and post-Nicene fathers wrote

against these gnostic heresies. Iraneus, Tertullian, Origen, Novatian, and Augustine were some of the fathers who began to find freedom to address doctrinal issues in a new era of peace for Christianity. However, much of the damage had been done, as gnostic philosophies had eaten its way like a cancer into the church, and could not be properly excised. Some of the writings against these heresies led to the establishment of the institutionalized Roman Catholic Church, with its papal head at the Church of Rome.

The spirit of antichrist, according to John, began early in the first century, bringing gnostic beliefs into the church. This is the spirit that was unleashed with the opening of the first seal in the form of the white horse and its rider. A study of history from the first century to the present shows indisputable evidence of this conquering, dominating spirit in the earth, using Christianity to introduce pagan influences and heretical doctrines into an institutionalized corporate church. But the spirit of antichrist need not be restricted only to Gnosticism. While the spirit was first made manifest within gnostic teaching, any religion, organization, hierarchy, or denomination that uses the name of Jesus Christ, Christianity, or the gospel to force, coerce, or brainwash its adherents is being led by the spirit of antichrist and religious domination symbolized within the first seal.

As stated above, Constantine's arrival brought about a major change in the Roman Empire's attitude toward Christianity. He revolted against Rome and took his power to Byzantium, later renamed Constantinople, which marked a split in the Roman Empire. The Edict of Milan, a joint effort of Constantine in the eastern branch of the empire and Licinius in the western branch, brought to an end the severe persecution of Christians and instituted freedom of religion, but also served to incorporate the worship of Greek and Roman gods into Christianity. Later, Emperor Theodosius decreed Catholic Christianity to be the state religion, ordering people to be labeled Catholics and judging those who fell outside their parameters as raving mad and worthy of whatever punishment the Roman Catholic Church could devise.

The result of the Edict of Milan and Theodosian decrees were forced conversions of pagans, causing churches to be filled with false converts. In response to the split of the Roman Empire from Rome by Constantine and others from the Western branch, the bishops of Rome established the papal hierarchy, featuring an earthly priesthood with bishops, cardinals, priests, and other ministers, with the Pontifex Maximus at the head, the Pope.

The Dominating Spirit of the Roman Catholic Church

The spirit of antichrist continued his conquering of the masses throughout the centuries and even into the present through this papal system within the Roman Catholic Church, the largest and most powerful religious order on the earth today. The Roman Catholic Church's persecution of underground Christianity throughout the centuries reveals the fruit of the spirit of domination that permeates the papacy's history. The statements below provide a select sampling of thousands of declarations by leaders of the Roman Catholic Church. These examples clearly show that the papal system has dominated the religious world ever since its foundation, requiring submission and obedience to its decrees by the universal corporate church as if they were uttered by Jesus Christ himself.

> I glorify you for having maintained your authority by putting to death those wandering sheep who refuse to enter the fold; and . . . congratulate you upon having opened the kingdom of heaven to the people submitted to your rule.
> A king need not fear to command massacres, when these will retain his subjects in obedience, or cause them to submit to the faith of Christ; and

God will reward him in this world, and in eternal
life, for these murders.[1]

- Pope Nicholas I (858-867) when encouraging the King of
Bulgaria to force Roman Catholicism on his subjects.

We desire to show the world that we can give or
take away at our will kingdoms, duchies,
earldoms, in a word, the possession of all men;
for we can bind and loose.[2]

- Pope Gregory VII (1073-1085) in the Roman Synod of 1080.

By the authority which God has given us in the
person of St. Peter, we declare you king, and we
order the people to render you, in this capacity,
homage and obedience. We, however, shall
expect you to subscribe to all our desires as a
return for the imperial crown[3]

- Pope Innocent III (1198-1216) in declaring Otho of
Saxony to be the king of Germany.

We hear that you forbid torture as contrary to the
laws of your land. But no state law can override
canon law, our law. Therefore I command you at
once to submit those men to torture.[4]

- Pope Clement V (1305-1314) to King Edward II of England
due to a revolt against papal power.

While there is still time, then, turn your forces
against Bohemia; burn, massacre, make deserts
everywhere, for nothing could be more agreeable
to God, or more useful to the cause of kings, than
the extermination of the Hussites.[5]

- Pope Martin V (1417-1431), who commanded the King of Poland to massacre the Hussites, who resisted in honor of Jan Hus, a martyr.

> It is not enough for the people only to know that the Pope is the head of the Church . . .they must also understand that their own faith and religious life flow from him; that in him is the bond which unites Catholics to one another, and the power which strengthens and the light which guides them; that he is the dispenser of spiritual graces, the giver of the benefits of religion, the upholder of justice, and the protector of the oppressed.[6]

- La Civilta Cattolica, or The Catholic Civilization.

> Each individual must receive the faith and law from the Church...with unquestioning submission and obedience of the intellect and the will...We have no right to ask reasons of the church, any more than of Almighty God...We are to take with unquestioning docility whatever instruction the Church gives us.[7]

- The Catholic World, in 1871, Vatican I Council.

While pondering these declarations, remember that what is symbolized within the first seal is the granting of permission in the spirit world to carry out the events within the seals. An antichrist spirit of religious domination, using the name of Christ, was unleashed to conquer the people and dominate their minds. This conquering began with Gnosticism being introduced in the first century, and a careful study of the history of the institutional church and the emergence of the papal system will reveal that both have their foundation in Gnosticism. Thus, there is a chain that connects the early gnostic heresies and the emergence of the papal system that has dominated the masses through religion for centuries. Such religious domination continues today despite the Protestant Reformation.

While the examples above focused on the Roman Catholic Church, there are many other groups, which have either in the past used, or are currently using, the name of Jesus Christ to conquer the minds of their adherents through deception and brainwashing. Even the modern New Age "gospel" arose from early Gnostic thought, using the name of "the Christ" to brainwash adherents into believing they have a divine Christ-self inside them to which they must ascend. The New Age falsely teaches there is a transition that everyone must eventually achieve, similar to what Jesus experienced in his life at his baptism and later ascension to heaven.

Consider the contrasting restraint evident throughout the ministry of Jesus Christ. He never forced or imposed himself on anyone, nor did he coerce, trick, or brainwash anyone into believing in his teaching. How much less compulsory could Jesus become than to declare that in order to follow him, a person had to pick up their cross every day? Picking up the cross meant, to the Jews of his day, the cross of crucifixion upon which many of their contemporaries had died at the hands of the oppressive Roman Empire. Jesus made it clear that to follow him would be a sacrifice.

The spirit at work within the first seal (symbolized by a white horse with a bow and crown) began its domination on the earth in the first century after Christ's finished work on the cross and ascension to God's right hand. It is still at work today in different fashions and within many different religious orders. The second, third, and fourth seals, and their comparison to the description Jesus provided in Matthew chapter 24 and Luke chapter 21, will be explored in the next chapter.

---

[1] De Cormenin, Louis Marie. *History of the Popes*, p. 243, as cited in R.W. Thompson (1876) *The Papacy and the Civil Power*, p. 244. New York.

[2] von Dollinger, J. H. Ignaz (1869), *The Pope and the Council,* pp. 87-89. London.

[3] De Cormenin, Louis Marie. *History of the Popes*, p. 243, as cited in R.W. Thompson (1876) *The Papacy and the Civil Power*, p. 459. New York.

[4] Durant, Will (1950). *The Story of Civilization*, vol. IV, p. 680. Simon and Schuster.

[5] De Cormenin, Louis Marie. *History of the Popes*, pp. 116-117, as cited in R.W. Thompson (1876) *The Papacy and the Civil Power*, p. 553. New York.

[6] La Civilta Cattolica, 1867, vol. Xii, p. 86.

[7] "The Catholic World", August 1871, vol. xiii, pp. 580-589.

8

Spirits of Physical And Economic Oppression

C ontinuing with the opening of the second, third, and fourth
seals, three more horses are granted authority to oppress
humanity. While the first seal represents a type of spiritual and
mental oppression of humanity, the second, third, and fourth
seals represent several types of physical and financial
oppression.

The Second Seal: A Spirit of Violence and Bloodshed
After the Lamb opened the first seal, the second seal was
opened. The symbols of the second seal are (1) a fiery red horse
and its rider, (2) a twofold mission to take peace from the earth
and cause people to brutally murder each other, and (3) a large
sword:

> Then when the Lamb opened the second seal, I
> heard the second living creature saying, "Come!"
> And another horse, fiery red, came out, and the

> one who rode it was granted permission to take peace from the earth, so that people would butcher one another [*spháxousin*], and he was given a huge sword. (*Rev 6:3-4*)

The first of the twofold mission of this spirit is to take peace from the earth. This deceptive power has no doubt resulted in the violence that we have seen in numerous wars since the first century. The history books are full of these wars, so a detailed study of them is not warranted in this book. But not only is the normal kind of violence and murder that takes place in territorial wars in view within this seal, but a special type of demonized violence that causes people to viciously torture and murder.

The more common Greek verb for "kill" in the New Testament is *apokteinō*, used 82 times in the New Testament. The root Greek word for "butcher" in verse 4, however, is *spházō*, a verb used to describe the act of slaughtering animals for sacrifice or food. It means to put to death in an extremely violent and merciless manner, but even more than that, without a conscience for the act. That is the context of this verb: to kill human beings with violence and without conscience. This verb is used sparingly throughout the New Testament, appearing only ten times in I John and Revelation.

This type of senseless, violent killing was definitely seen under the brutal rule of Nero in the first century, and continued throughout the rules of many of the Roman Emperors. Christians were killed for sport, and without conscience. This type of murder continued throughout the centuries with the Crusades and the various Inquisitions. In addition, wars of "ethnic cleansing" in Europe, Asia, and other parts of the world have raged for centuries, and continue to the present.

Jesus prophesied the type of violence described in the second seal. He called them the beginning of the birth pains in Matthew chapter 24 along with wars, rumors of wars, nations and kingdoms rising against each other, and the killing of believers. As for the symbol of the sword, in the Old Testament, the sword was routinely used as a metaphor for war and violence. The sword symbolized the threat of invading armies against the Israelites. Similarly, the sword of the second seal symbolizes the use of force and violence to kill humanity throughout the centuries.

The Third Seal Yoke of Bondage
John heard the third living creature call out, and the Lamb opened the third seal. The symbols of the third seal are (1) a black horse and its rider, (2) a yoke, or *zugón* in Greek, in his hand, and (3) an oppressive declaration and command concerning food and money:

> Then when the Lamb opened the third seal I heard the third living creature saying, "Come!" So I looked, and here came a black horse! The one who rode it had a balance scale [*zugón*] in his hand. Then I heard something like a voice from among the four living creatures saying, "A quart of wheat will cost a day's pay and three quarts of barley will cost a day's pay. But do not damage the olive oil and the wine!" (*Rev 6:5-6*)

The object this rider held in his hand must be explored in order to understand the meaning of this seal. Almost every translation and paraphrase of the Bible examined in preparation of this book rendered the Greek noun *zugós* as a pair of balances, or a balance scale. The noun *zugós* has other meanings, but the reason provided for translating it as a balance scale is the language of the verse that follows, which speaks of the price for certain measurements of grain and barley. The common interpretation has been that food will be measured out and scarce, and rationing necessary, and therefore what the rider holds must be a balance scale. In the Septuagint Greek translation of the Old Testament, the noun *zugós* was translated many times as a balance scale, including the following verses:

> You shall not act unrighteously in judgment, in measures and weights and scales [*zugói*]. (*Lev 19:35*)

> Who has measured the water in His hand, and the heaven with a span, and all the earth in a handful? Who has weighed the mountains in scales, and the forests in a balance [*zugó*]? (*Isa 40:12*)

However, the primary definition of *zugós* or *zugón* in the Septuagint Old Testament, and the Greek New Testament, is a yoke that is used to bind two or more cattle together for plowing. The metaphorical meaning of the word is burden or bondage, and was often used in the Old Testament to describe the burdensome Mosaic laws. In fact, *zugós* comes from the root word *zeúgnumi*, which means to join or bind together. In each New Testament usage of this noun, other than Revelation chapter 6, *zugón* is translated as "yoke" with a context of burden or oppression, including these passages:

> Take my yoke [*zugón*] on you and learn from me, because I am gentle and humble in heart, and you will find rest for your souls. For my yoke [*zugós*] is easy to bear, and my load is not hard to carry." (*Mat 11:29-30*)

> So now why are you putting God to the test by placing on the neck of the disciples a yoke [*zugón*] that neither our ancestors nor we have been able to bear? (*Act 15:10*)

> For freedom Christ has set us free. Stand firm,
> then, and do not be subject again to the yoke
> [*zugó*] of slavery. (*Gal 5:1*)

Jesus explained his yoke or burden was easy to bear. The disciples in Acts described the prescriptions of the law of Moses as a proverbial yoke around their necks. In Galatians, Paul referred to the yoke of slavery. These verses provide guidance about the meaning of the *zugón* in the hand of the black horse rider: a symbolism of a certain kind of bondage and oppression. The traditional interpretation that the *zugón* must be a balance scale representing famine and rationing of food is further weakened by the fact that the fourth seal specifically mentions famine. Why would the third and fourth seals both specifically refer to famine?

A clue about the type of bondage this seal represents is found within Revelation 6:6. The voice heard speaking about the rider and the balance scale in its hand mentions the cost of the staples of first century life: wheat, barley, olive oil, and wine. Thus, it can be concluded that the meaning of the symbolism of the third seal is a spirit of financial bondage and oppression that was sent out into the earth. Some possibilities of the kind of financial oppression that this horse and rider represent, based on the message that emerged from among the four living creatures, include:

1. Price controls on the necessities of life, such as food.
2. Inflation and hyperinflation in the price of goods.
3. Scarcity of the necessities of life due to controls on production.
4. Efforts by governing authorities to exercise control over the value of currencies.
5. Efforts by governing authorities to expand or contract the supply of money.

History is full of examples of all of these types economic controls, such as the Roman Empire as it began its slow decline. Since that decline, other empires have experimented with many of these economic controls. Some prospered for a while, but most failed miserably. The consequences of the failures have historically been borne by the common person in the form of lost wealth, scarcity of goods, oppressive taxation, or insurmountable debt.

Perhaps the greatest success story since the fall of the Roman Empire has been the United States of America. Currently, through a series of changes in monetary policy and Constitutional amendments, the United States has inflated the price of its goods many times over, and is multi-trillions of dollars in debt to the privately-held Federal Reserve with no hard asset backing its paper money. A financial meltdown is imminent, and if history is to repeat, the citizenry will again bear the undesirable consequences. Consider these incredibly insightful words from Thomas Jefferson in 1816, one of the founding fathers of the United States, about excessive indebtedness:

> We must not let our rulers load us with perpetual debt. We must make our election between economy and liberty or profusion and servitude.

> If we run into such debt, as that we must be taxed in our meat and in our drink, in our necessaries and our comforts, in our labors and our amusements, for our calling and our creeds... [we will] have no time to think, no means of calling our miss-managers to account, but be glad to obtain subsistence by hiring ourselves to rivet their chains on the necks of our fellow-

sufferers...And this is the tendency of all human governments.

A departure from principle in one instance becomes a precedent for [another]...till the bulk of society is reduced to be mere automatons of misery...And the fore-horse of this frightful team is public debt. Taxation follows that, and in its train wretchedness and oppression.[1]

Jefferson referred to chains on the necks of the citizenry, and their eventual debasement to mere automatons of misery: a perfect representation of the oppressive yoke around the neck of a beast of burden, and a poignant picture of what is symbolized in the third seal. Jefferson spoke from experience, warning the other founders that following the policies that led to past failures will lead to an enchained populace. Time has proven Jefferson to be correct, and it remains to be seen what will become of the United States.

From the first century until the present, a spirit has been at work to wreak havoc on the economies of the world. Injustice, oppression, and inequity are the goals, and the tools have been governments who have implemented unsound economic controls and unjust taxation through their laws. The underlying reason? Greed. The love of money and the desire to accumulate wealth no matter the cost. That is the spirit symbolized by the black horse and rider, holding a yoke in his hand to represent bondage and oppression of the people.

The Fourth Seal: Death and Hades
John heard the fourth and final living creature call out, and the Lamb opened the fourth seal. The symbols of the fourth seal are (1) a pale green horse, (2) a rider with the name Death, (3) a follower of the rider named Hades, and (4) authority to kill a

quarter of the earth's population with four different types of physical oppression:

> Then when the Lamb opened the fourth seal I heard the voice of the fourth living creature saying, "Come!" So I looked and here came a pale green horse! The name of the one who rode it was Death [*Thánatos*], and Hades followed right behind. They were given [*edothē*] authority over a fourth of the earth, to kill its population with the sword, famine, and disease, and by the wild animals of the earth. (*Rev 6:7-8*)

This spirit was granted its authority to kill with the sword, with famine, with diseases, and with beasts of the earth. History, of course, is full of examples of these kinds of things occurring both before and after the incarnation of Christ on earth. However, this was a specific granting of authority at the opening of the fourth seal, just after the ascension of Jesus Christ to God's right hand.

The first method of judgment, the sword, was discussed within the second seal red horse. It symbolizes war and violence throughout the Bible, but its mention within the fourth seal may represent a general spirit of violence and murder in the earth outside of wars. The second method of judgment, famine or hunger, is another way this spirit of death has authority to kill one-fourth of the population. Famine has been a major killer of humanity on every populated continent, especially more recently in Africa and Asia in such countries as Cambodia, Thailand, Bangladesh, Ethiopia, Zimbabwe, Russia, Sudan, Somalia, India, and others.

The third method of judgment, disease, is actually "death" or *thánatos* in Greek. Disease, plague, and pestilence have resulted in much devastation on the earth. History is full of examples of plagues which have taken the lives of millions over the centuries. The fourth method of judgment, the beasts of the earth, may have the most stealth interpretation of the four. Notwithstanding the many examples of wild beasts killing humans throughout the centuries, the most convincing candidate for death being dealt to humanity through the wild beasts of the earth is the microscopic bacteria that are carried in livestock, such as cattle and pigs, from which humanity gets the majority of the meat and dairy products it consumes. Perhaps this deeper meaning of the "beasts of the earth" has merit. To assume that the beasts of the earth are only larger animals that attack may be too narrow a focus. There are billions of germs and viruses that have the ability to kill humans, including viruses that have been genetically engineered by human beings as biological weapons.

Consider these interpretations within the framework of the other chapters within Revelation, as well as within the framework of other scriptures. In the famous discourse on the Mount of Olives, Jesus prophesied of the events that would occur throughout history, and they are embodied within the first five seals of Revelation chapter 6. The next chapter is an important one, in which the fifth seal and the importance of the laws against the shedding of innocent blood will be explored. There will come a point in the future when the cup of God's wrath is full due to the blood of the innocent and martyrs of Christ shed on the earth. The earth will be cleansed of the guilt of shedding of innocent blood in preparation for Christ's reign on the earth.

---

[1] Letter of Thomas Jefferson to Samuel Kercheval, Monticello, July 12, 1816.

9

FIFTH SEAL: SHEDDING INNOCENT BLOOD

W ithin the verses that comprise the description of the fifth seal, an important clue is revealed concerning when the future three-stage translation event will occur. Rather than a date, it is the completion of a prophesied period of time of persecution against believers. This chapter will also include an important investigation of what the Word of God says about the shedding of innocent blood, and the judgment that ensues as a result. At the conclusion of the chapter, the overarching purpose of the horrific judgments during the day of the Lord's wrath will become completely clear.

Under the Heavenly Altar of Incense
There is an important transition at the beginning of Revelation 6:9. The first four seals feature the four horses in symbolism, while the fifth seal features more concrete and literal descriptions. No doubt John was still seeing a vision of the

"hereafter," or the things that were to happen "after these things," but the vision moved from using strict symbolism to literal persons and places. Note what John saw when the Lamb opened the fifth seal:

> Now when the Lamb opened the fifth seal, I saw under the altar the souls of those who had been violently killed because of the word of God and because of the testimony they had given. They cried out with a loud voice, "How long, Sovereign Master, holy and true, before you judge those who live on the earth and avenge our blood?" Each of them was given a long white robe and they were told to rest for a little longer, until the full number was reached of both their fellow servants and their brothers who were going to be killed just as they had been. (*Rev 6:9-11*)

The most striking characteristic separating the first four seals from the fifth seal is that the opening of the fifth seal did not set loose a spiritual force to wreak havoc on the earth. Instead, it was to show John the souls that had been and would be killed for their faith in Jesus Christ, and that their cry would not be answered until their full number reached. Note that the souls of the individuals John saw were under the altar. According to Revelation chapter 9, this altar is located directly before God's throne. Therefore, the cry of the innocent blood from the martyrs, murdered for their Christian testimony, is a constant reminder before God of their innocent blood shed on the earth, and of the vengeance to be meted on their behalf.

How Long?

The cry of those who suffered a violent death on earth is a question. They want to know how much more time would pass before their innocent blood will be avenged on the earth. This is a strange question if these are martyrs who will be killed by the future beast system. In addition to the rest of the evidence to be explored later in this chapter, there are three convincing reasons that provide confirmation that these martyrs will not be asking this question *after* the day of the Lord's wrath.

First, if these represent martyrs which will be beheaded by the beast for refusing to take the mark of the beast, as the traditional pre-millennial interpretation of these martyrs suggests, then why would they cry out for the avenging of their blood *after* the day of the Lord's wrath would have already begun? After the mark of the beast has been implemented, the first six trumpet judgments will have been unleashed, which would mean that martyrs would be crying out for the Lord's vengeance *after* the Lord's vengeance had already begun.

Second, if these represent martyrs violently killed during the day of the Lord's wrath, why would they be asking "How long" if the length of the day of the Lord's wrath is already known? If the day of the Lord's wrath lasts three and one half years, and these martyrs were killed several months into this time frame, they would know how much time remained. There would be no need to ask this question.

Third, if these souls represent martyrs beheaded during the day of the Lord's wrath, they are getting impatient very quickly, because they will have only been seeking vengeance for a few short years. Their question gives off the impression that they have been crying out for revenge for a prolonged period of time. On the other hand, if this vision is representative of the throne room scene from the beginning of the first century persecution and martyrdom until the time before the sixth seal, as this prophetic model holds, then these martyrs have been waiting for hundreds, perhaps thousands of years for their deaths to be avenged.

In addition, no harm is done to the chronological flow of

Revelation. The placement of the events of the fifth seal near the end of "Daniel's 70th week" under the traditional pre-millennial view is out of order with respect to the trumpet judgments, the two witnesses, the beast and his mark, the image of the beast, the false prophet, and the bowl judgments within the chronological flow of Revelation.

There *will* be a group of believers who, during the day of the Lord's wrath, will be killed in a violent manner for their testimony about Jesus and the Word of God:

> . . . I also saw the souls of those who had been beheaded because of the testimony about Jesus and because of the word of God. These had not worshiped the beast or his image and had refused to receive his mark . . . (*Rev 20:4*)

Therefore, even *after* the full number of Christian martyrs is reached in the fifth seal, these individuals will also be violently beheaded for their testimony. However, this is a group of saints who are separate from the resurrected and caught-up body of Christ; a group whom Revelation 13:7 reveals that the beast is allowed to conquer or overcome. This group of beheaded martyrs during the day of the Lord's wrath are specifically referred to in Revelation chapter 15 as a separate group from the vast throng of believers which had *already* been resurrected and caught up to heaven:

> Then I saw something like a sea of glass mixed with fire, and those who had conquered the beast and his image and the number of his name. They were standing by the sea of glass, holding harps given to them by God. (*Rev 15:2*)

They will be killed during the 42-month reign of the beast after the establishment of the mark of the beast, at a specific time in the future, rather than over the centuries. Because of their separate mention in Revelation chapters 15 and 20, their specified time of persecution and murder during the 42-month reign of the beast, and the additional three reasons stated above, the beheaded martyrs of the day of the Lord's wrath are not in view in the description of the fifth seal.

The answer given to the fifth seal martyrs as to how long they must wait for the Lord's vengeance is equally revealing. They were told to wait until a "full number was reached" of other Christians who would be killed using the same violence with which they were killed. The word "until" is key, because it signifies that there will come a point when the cry from underneath the altar becomes so loud that God can no longer bear to allow their blood to go without revenge. At some point, there will come one final martyr who tips the scales of God's patience, and that "full number" is finally reached. Until that point, these martyrs continue to cry underneath the altar before God.

The responsibility for the shedding of innocent blood in the earth is revealed in Revelation chapter 18 as Babylon, a term symbolizing a pseudo-religious and economic machine that has taken over the entire earth. This judgment on Babylon is meted out during the day of the Lord's wrath. God currently waits in his mercy for mankind to repent from its rebellion and turn back to him. For now, his wrath for the shedding of innocent blood is withheld despite the cry of the martyrs under the altar. However, there will come a time when the final martyr is murdered and the full number is finally reached. Horrible deaths will occur, yet those deaths must occur in order for the completion of the age of God's grace and mercy to come.

The Laws against Shedding Innocent Blood
When God handed down his laws to Moses, he set forth detailed laws on intentional murder, accidental murder, and unsolved

homicide. Some of the laws are very strange, and don't seem to make a lot of sense unless it is understood that the land becomes polluted when innocent blood is shed upon it. Remember what God told Cain after he murdered his brother Abel:

> But the Lord said, "What have you done? The voice of your brother's blood is crying out to me from the ground! So now, you are banished from the ground, which has opened its mouth to receive your brother's blood from your hand. *(Gen 4:10-11)*

Blood has a voice when it is shed innocently in the earth. The lifeblood of that person, and all the offspring that would have been born from that person, are cut off from existence. When innocent blood is shed, it cries out from the ground to be avenged. Although God revealed the laws concerning murder to Moses, he first established his precepts regarding the shedding of blood to Noah just after the flood:

> For your lifeblood I will surely exact punishment, from every living creature I will exact punishment. From each person I will exact punishment for the life of the individual since the man was his relative. "Whoever sheds human blood, by other humans must his blood be shed; for in God's image God has made mankind." *(Gen 9:5-6)*

The shedding of innocent blood was a serious thing to the Lord, requiring several laws to be established regarding its judgment and punishment. Before the children of Israel were to inherit the Promised Land, the Lord instructed Moses to set aside three cities of refuge for someone who accidentally kills another person whom he does not hate at the time of the act. However, in the case of an intentional murder, the elders of the city in which the murder was committed were to have that man face the avenger of blood. Then, the murderer was to be killed for his capital crime by his avenger:

> The avenger of blood himself must kill the murderer; when he meets him, he must kill him. Moreover, you must not accept a ransom for the life of a murderer who is guilty of death; he must surely be put to death. (*Num 35:19; 31*)

One reason this law was established was to deter humans from murder. Not even a ransom for the life of a murderer could be accepted. But the primary reason why the Lord established the law of capital punishment is that the blood of the innocent must be purged from the land by shedding the blood of the guilty. This would result in a land free from defilement of guilt, and it would go well with the inhabitants of that particular land:

> You must not pity him, but purge out the blood of the innocent from Israel, so that it may go well with you. (*Deu 19:13*)

> "You must not pollute the land where you live, for blood defiles the land, and the land cannot be cleansed of the blood that is shed there, except by the blood of the person who shed it. (*Num 35:33*)

Is all of this just poetic? Does blood truly cry out for vengeance from the ground, and does the shedding of guilty blood actually have some kind of spiritual cleansing effect on the land? God took very seriously the cleansing of the land of the guilt of shedding the blood of the innocent, as should the student of prophecy. What conclusions can be drawn so far from this information?

1. The shedding of innocent blood both pollutes and defiles the land in which it is shed.
2. The guilt of shedding innocent blood must be purged from the land in which it is shed.
3. In order to purge the innocent blood from the land in which it is shed, the blood of the murderer must also be shed.
4. If the blood of the innocent is not purged from the land, the land will remain defiled and things will not go well for its inhabitants.

Combine these conclusions with the picture of the innocent martyrs under the altar before the Lord, crying out for vengeance of their shed blood, and the picture begins to become even more vivid. Their innocent blood was not avenged with the blood of their murderers, therefore, the land in which their blood was shed is defiled and their blood continues to cry out for vengeance.

A prime example of this can be found in the life of Manasseh, former king of Israel. In addition to setting up the worship of idols in Israel, he shed the blood of many innocent people. According to II Kings chapters 21 and 24, Manasseh stained Jerusalem with the blood of innocent people from one end to the other. The Lord promised to punish this sin by bringing judgment against the land and its inhabitants, not against Manasseh or his family. Because the blood of the innocent killed by Manasseh was not purged with the blood of the murderers, as the laws God laws initially established required, judgment came on the land. The Psalmist, in recounting the sordid history of the Israelites from their deliverance from the Egyptians until the reign of King David, records the incredible depravity to which they stooped:

> They sacrificed their sons and daughters to demons. They shed innocent blood—the blood of

their sons and daughters, whom they sacrificed to the idols of Canaan. The land was polluted by bloodshed. (*Psa 106:37-38*)

The Psalmist here simply applied the laws handed down to Moses and later recorded in Numbers and Deuteronomy. The blood of innocent people was shed and the land was therefore polluted as a result. Another example of the consequences of the shedding of innocent blood is recorded in Joel chapter 3 with a judgment of desolation against Egypt and Edom:

Egypt will be desolate and Edom will be a desolate wilderness, because of the violence they did to the people of Judah, in whose land they shed innocent blood. (*Joe 3:19*)

Once again, the judgments for the shedding of innocent blood came on the land. Notice that the lands of both Egypt and Edom were to become desolate due to the shedding of the innocent blood of the Judeans. In the process of this desolation, the people that were residing in those lands would also feel the effects of the desolation, but the primary reason for the judgment is to make the land desolate so that it could be purged of the guilt of shedding innocent blood.

Laws Concerning Unsolved Murders

Another very interesting law was established by the Lord in the case of a victim of a homicide that no one witnessed. Imagine that a victim was found in the land of Israel, and no one knew how that person died. In such a case, the elders and judges of the surrounding cities were to measure from their city to the victim, and the closest city to the victim was to perform a strange ceremony. A heifer that had never worn a yoke to work was to be brought to a valley which had water flowing through it and which had never been plowed or sown for crops. The Levitical priests were to be present to observe the proceedings. Once these conditions were met, the heifer was to be taken down to the water, and the elders and judges were to break its neck over the water. Then, the elders were to wash their hands with the water in the valley over the neck of the heifer that had just been broken. As they were washing their hands:

> Then they must proclaim, "Our hands have not spilled this blood, nor have we witnessed the crime. Do not blame your people Israel whom you redeemed, O Lord, and do not hold them accountable for the bloodshed of an innocent person." Then atonement will be made for the bloodshed. (*Deu 21:7-8*)

The purpose of the ceremony was to make atonement for the shedding of the innocent blood in the land. As with the other set of laws, the blood is purged from the land, but in this case, by the blood of the heifer since the actual murderer was unknown.

It appears that Pontius Pilate may have known about these laws. When Jesus stood innocent before his accusers at his arrest and scourging, the Jews called for his crucifixion over and over. Pilate's final response was to wash his hands with water before the crowd and declare himself innocent of Jesus' blood. Pilate was attempting to purge the guilt of innocent blood from his hands, just as described in Deuteronomy chapter 21 with the washing of hands over the heifer. He declared himself to be innocent of the blood of Jesus Christ, an innocent man. The Jews then cried out a response to this act of hand washing, because they themselves knew the law with which Pilate was attempting to abdicate himself: "Let his blood be on us and on our children!"

The Blood of the Martyrs

After the death and resurrection of Jesus Christ, there seemed to be no type of torture or death that could dissuade his fearless followers from proclaiming the gospel in every part of the populated world. The first martyrdom on record is the dramatic stoning of Stephen, a man full of faith and the anointing of the Holy Spirit. Stephen's martyrdom spawned a great persecution against the church in Jerusalem, and Saul of Tarsus was a major part of it. After his dramatic conversion and name change to Paul, he himself was beheaded under the persecution of Nero. The blood of the martyrs continued to be shed throughout the centuries, with millions of Christians feeling the crush of the murderous power of the institutional "church," including the Waldenses in France, the Anabaptists, the Hussites, the Moravians, and others. The murder continues even today in foreign nations as missionaries and underground believers give their lives for Christ.

The guilt of the innocent blood must be purged from the land, and if God is a God of justice, he will exact the same judgment on the land that he did in the previous examples. God stated that vengeance belongs to him, and he will ensure the land is cleansed of the guilt of shedding innocent blood. The martyrs of the fifth seal asked how long it would be before their innocent blood was avenged. The answer they received was the conclusion of long period of bloodshed, when the full number is reached of their fellow brothers in Christ who would be killed in the same manner as they were. After the full number of Christian martyrs is finally reached, the events of the sixth seal will begin, which will accompany the translation process of all believers, to be followed afterward by the day of the Lord's wrath. At that point, the shedding of the innocent blood of the martyrs of the church will come to an end, and the day of the Lord's wrath will begin. This will be declared by those on the earth after the sixth seal events take place:

> They said to the mountains and to the rocks, "Fall
> on us and hide us from the face of the one who is
> seated on the throne and from the wrath of the
> Lamb, because the great day of their wrath has
> come, and who is able to withstand it?" (*Rev
> 6:16-17*)

Recall the principles stated earlier in this chapter and realize
that the blood of the guilty was the only thing that was able to
cleanse the land of the guilt of the innocent blood shed within it.
This means that the earth is *currently* in a state of defilement
because the blood of the guilty has not been shed to cleanse it.
During the day of the Lord's wrath, he will provide a
supernatural source of blood. The prophet Isaiah foretold of the
time of God's vengeance:

> Go, my people! Enter your inner rooms! Close
> your doors behind you! Hide for a little while,
> until his angry judgment is over! For look, the
> Lord is coming out of the place where he lives, to
> punish the sin of those who live on the earth. The
> earth will display the blood shed on it; it will no
> longer cover up its slain. (*Isa 26:20-21*)

These verses, read in connection with the idea of the
cleansing of the defiled earth due to the shedding of innocent
blood, concisely tie four important concepts of this prophetic
model together:

1. There will be a group of persons, the "my people" of the
   Isaiah passage, who are hidden in the inner rooms when the
   Lord's anger is unleashed on the earth. This represents the
   catching up of all believers from the earth prior to the day of
   the Lord's wrath.

2. The day of the Lord's wrath will begin *after* this group of people is hidden away, and will take place *while* they are hidden away.

3. The purpose of the unleashing of the Lord's wrath will be to *cleanse the guilt* of shedding innocent blood on the earth. The slain martyrs will finally receive their vengeance.

4. Something will take place on the earth such that the blood shed on it will be on display; no longer will the blood of the innocent be hidden. This is a reference not only to the blood judgments of Revelation chapters 8 and 16, but also to an event that will trigger a time when blood, before hidden, will no longer be hidden. This triggering event is the future three-stage translation of believers amidst the great shaking and the other effects of the sixth seal.

In addition, the preceding verse to the Isaiah passage above ties in a fifth important concept of this prophetic model:

> Your dead will come back to life; your corpses will rise up. Wake up and shout joyfully, you who live in the ground! For you will grow like plants drenched with the morning dew, and the earth will bring forth its dead spirits. (*Isa 26:19*)

5. There will be a resurrection of the dead in Christ, and that resurrection will precede the catching up of living believers. Note that the dead come to life first, followed by the people being shut up in the inner room in verse 20.

This is a key passage in understanding the timing of the future translation of believers within the Revelation chronology. Without question, these verses make it clear that the people of God will enter an "inner room," with the door closed behind them. How long are they hidden? For a little while, until the judgment on the earth is over, a reference to the day of the Lord's wrath in the future. Take special note that the Lord's judgment does not happen *until* his people are hidden away, and that the judgment happens *while* they are hidden away.

The Judgments Involve Blood

Beginning with the first judgment within the day of the Lord's wrath, blood is involved. The first angel will blow its trumpet, and blood will be mixed into fire and hail that will burn up one-third of the earth, one-third of all trees, and all of the green grass. The blood will be cleansing the land of the guilt of shedding innocent blood. In the second trumpet judgment, as a result of a great burning mountain crashing into the sea, one-third of the sea will turn into blood. Again, blood will be purging the land of the guilt that defiles it. Later, the bowl judgments will take place and are even more severe than the trumpet judgments. All of the seas, the rivers, and the springs will turn into blood, killing every living sea creature, whereas with the second trumpet judgment, only one-third of the sea turns into blood. Imagine the devastation from all of the seas and rivers on the earth turning to blood, killing the sea creatures. Could all this be a part of the cleansing process for the guilt of shedding innocent blood? Take note of the explanation of the purpose of these two bowl judgments:

> Now I heard the angel of the waters saying: "You are just—the one who is and who was, the Holy One—because you have passed these judgments, because they poured out the blood of your saints and prophets, so you have given them blood to drink. They got what they deserved!" (*Rev 16:5-6*)

The righteous justice of the Lord is seen in pouring out the judgments during the day of his wrath. The guilt of the blood of the innocent has defiled the earth without recourse. If Jesus Christ is returning to reign on the earth, should he be expected to reign on a land that is completely defiled, contaminated with the guilt of shedding innocent blood? The cleansing of the earth is paramount through the judgments of the day of the Lord's wrath, evidenced by the blood poured out and the destruction of the land. This is an overarching purpose for the blood poured out during the trumpet and bowl judgments.

The justice will be poured out all at once, and the angel even declared that the inhabitants of the earth are getting what they deserve by being given blood to drink through the waters being turned to blood. But the next verse is even more revealing:

> Then I heard *the altar* reply, "Yes, Lord God, the All-Powerful, your judgments are true and just!" (*Rev 16:7*)

The origin of this statement is the altar where the souls of the martyrs, earlier seen by John, are gathered underneath and crying out for vengeance. Here, the altar itself declared that the Lord is both true and just in pouring out blood on the earth. Remember who were located under the altar as revealed in the fifth seal? The martyrs who were crying out for vengeance for the shedding of the innocent blood! This is a powerful connection between the altar, the blood of the innocent, and God's wrath involving blood. It provides confirmation that the martyred souls under the altar had finally received the vengeance that they requested for so long.

Further proof that this will be a time when God pours out vengeance specifically for the shedding of innocent blood is found within the closing chapters of Revelation. Babylon is held responsible for the shedding of innocent blood on the earth:

> On her forehead was written a name, a mystery: "Babylon the Great, the Mother of prostitutes and of the detestable things of the earth." I saw that the woman was drunk with the blood of the saints and the blood of those who testified to Jesus. I was greatly astounded when I saw her. (*Rev 17:5-6*)

John was astounded because the woman was called Babylon, not the beast she was riding. The woman symbolized the pseudo-religious orders throughout history responsible for shedding the blood of the martyrs who testified of Jesus. Whether the Jews of the first century, the idolatrous Roman Empire, or the papal hierarchy for hundreds of years after them, all are a part of the religious arm of "Babylon the Great." In attempting to set up ways to get man back to God, the woman shunned God's attempt to reconcile humanity back to God through Jesus Christ and murdered those who tried to declare that message:

> because his judgments are true and just. For he has judged the great prostitute who corrupted the earth with her sexual immorality, and has avenged [*exedikēsen*] the blood [*haíma*] of his servants poured out by her own hands!" (*Rev 19:2*)

Note that God "avenged the blood" of the servants. This is exactly what the fifth seal martyrs were crying out for over the centuries:

> They cried out with a loud voice, "How long, Sovereign Master, holy and true, before you judge those who live on the earth and avenge [*ékdikeis*] our blood [*haíma*]?" (*Rev 6:10*)

The cry of the martyrs was to avenge their blood, and that is exactly what will happen with the judgments poured out in the Lord's wrath upon Babylon. This is the most convincing proof that the fifth seal martyrs are not those killed during the day of the Lord's wrath, but rather those killed over the centuries since the ascension of Jesus Christ to heaven. Those who hold that the opening of the seals will occur during the day of the Lord's wrath are forced to interpret the fifth seal as being only martyrs killed during the day of the Lord's wrath. For the many reasons established in this chapter, that is not a valid interpretation. Instead, for centuries these martyrs have been crying out for vengeance, and their request will be answered during that horrific period of the Lord's vengeance.

The end of the fifth seal, whenever that time arrives, marks a major turning point in history. When the blood of the final martyr has been shed, the day of the Lord's wrath will begin. It is necessary to understand the Old Testament laws against shedding innocent blood, and why God went to such lengths to set up laws to make sure the guilt of shedding innocent blood was purged from the land in which it was shed. This should aid in understanding the cry of the martyrs of the fifth seal, as well as the reason for the judgments of blood that will be poured out during the day of the Lord's wrath. The next chapter will feature an exploration of John's vision of the innumerable group of people around the throne of God whom one of the elders declared had departed great persecution, affliction, and suffering on the earth.

10

COMING OUT OF GREAT TRIBULATION

With the progression through Revelation chapters 4 through 6 now complete, it is time to move into Revelation chapter 7. The following events will have taken place prior to the events described in Revelation chapter 7:

1. The first four seals will have been broken, and the spirits granted authority in those seals influence and oppress mankind from the first century until the present. (Rev 6:1-8)
2. The full number of Gentile believers will have been grafted into the new covenant. (Rom 11:25)
3. The full number of martyrs will have just been reached, with the murder of the final pre-sixth seal believers. (Rev 6:11)
4. The resurrection of the dead in Christ. (I The 4:16-17; I Cor 15:51-53; Isa 26:19-20)
5. The transformation to immortality of the bodies of the resurrected dead in Christ and living believers. (I Cor 15:51-53; Phi 3:20-21)

6. The sudden catching up of all believers in transformed immortal bodies into the air to meet the Lord. (I The 4:16-17; Isa 26:19-20)

7. The sixth seal events, including the movement of all mountains and islands, a massive shaking of the earth, signs in the sun, moon, and sky, and possible magnetic or crustal pole shift. (Rev 6:12-14)

8. The day of the Lord's wrath will begin on the earth, according to the declaration of the people on the earth, after the sixth seal events. The blood of the innocent will be avenged. (Rev 6:16-17, 16:5-6; Isa 26:21)

The Innumerable Group before the Throne

In Revelation chapter 7, John is shown two separate visions: on the earth, a group of 144,000 descendants of the children of Israel who are sealed with the seal of the living God, and in heaven, a massive and innumerable group of people before the throne. The 144,000 are apparently literal persons descended from the line of Jacob, and represent a re-grafting of the broken branches of Israel into the cultivated olive tree of the faith, as Paul described in Romans chapter 11. But it is the innumerable group of people before the throne in heaven with which this chapter is concerned, which John described as follows:

> After these things I looked, and here was an enormous crowd that no one could count, made up of persons from every nation, tribe, people, and language, standing before the throne and before the Lamb dressed in long white robes, and with palm branches in their hands. (*Rev 7:9*)

First, identification of who makes up this group. In light of the model being proposed, which is focused on a shaking of the earth and the heavens at the resurrection of the dead in Christ at the opening of the sixth seal, and the catching up of all believers, it follows that this enormous group of people would be the translated group of believers, having just arrived in heaven in Revelation chapter 7.

This innumerable group appears nowhere else in Revelation, and is much too large to be made up solely of martyrs during the day of the Lord's wrath. According to Revelation chapter 20, those who refuse to worship the beast or its image, and refuse to receive the mark, will be killed by beheading and will not be resurrected until after the return of Jesus Christ in Revelation chapter 19:

> . . . I also saw the souls of those who had been beheaded because of the testimony about Jesus and because of the word of God. These had not worshiped the beast or his image and had refused to receive his mark on their forehead or hand. They came to life and reigned with Christ for a thousand years. (*Rev 20:4*)

It is interesting that the "people" of Revelation 7:9 are also associated with nations, tribes, and languages. This same particular foursome–nation, tribe, people, and language–are found three other times within Revelation: 11:9, 13:7, and 14:6. In each case, the author is referring to living people on the earth, and the same Greek words are used in the other three occurrences. For this reason, the "people" of Revelation 7:9 must be living, resurrected human beings, not the souls of martyrs who have not yet been resurrected.

In Revelation chapter 15, John described who he saw before the heavenly sea of glass:

> Then I saw something like a sea of glass mixed with fire, and those who had conquered the beast

and his image and the number of his name. They
were standing by the sea of glass, holding harps
given to them by God. (*Rev 15:2*)

How will these people "conquer" the beast, his image, and the
number of his name? By refusing to worship the beast or his
image and refusing to take his mark, which will result in being
beheaded. So, John saw this group of beast conquerors in the
heavenly realm, but later he revealed in Revelation 20:4 that
they are not to be resurrected from the dead until after the return
of Jesus Christ to reign on the earth. Therefore, what John sees
in Revelation chapter 15 must be the *souls* of the martyrs killed
during the day of the Lord's wrath. When they come to life, they
will reign with Christ 1,000 years. This 1,000-year period will
begin after Christ and his armies destroy the dragon, the beast,
and the false prophet.

Take note of the revealing contrast between the group before
the throne in Revelation chapter 7 and the group around the sea
of glass in Revelation chapter 15. The group in chapter 7 is
called "enormous" and "no one could count" their number.
Furthermore, they are described as "people." However, no
mention is made of the size of the group in chapter 15, and it is
certain they are not resurrected "people," since Revelation
chapter 20 reveals they will not be resurrected until the
beginning of the 1000-year period.

In addition, why would John be shown the same group of
martyrs in two different visions in chapters 7 and 15, one before
the beast is revealed, and one after the beast is revealed? Why
would they be described as enormous and innumerable in one
part of the vision, but be devoid of description in another part of
the vision? Why even refer to them twice? The answer to these
questions is that two separate groups are in view: the Revelation
chapter 7 group is the translated group of believers who appear
before the throne just after the events of the sixth seal, while the

Revelation chapter 15 group is the souls of those who are beheaded during the latter stages of the day of the Lord's wrath.

The appearance of this massive group of people around the throne in heaven in Revelation chapter 7, after the events of the sixth seal have taken place, is an absolutely perfect place for them to be introduced within the chronology of the visions of Revelation. If indeed the future resurrection, transformation, and catching-up event will occur within the events of the sixth seal, one would expect to see an innumerable crowd of people in their transformed and immortal bodies with the Lord in heaven at precisely the point at which they appear in Revelation chapter 7.

The enormity of this group is explained in that it includes countless believers throughout history over all the face of the earth, added to the vast number of Christians alive on this planet today. This would result in an "enormous crowd that no one could count," just as John described in the vision. That is indeed what is pictured in this verse. Looking back through Revelation chapters 4 through 7, this is the *only* reference to an enormous group of people in heaven, made up of all the nations of the earth, which could be identified with the resurrected and caught-up group of believers.

They Came Out Of The Great Tribulation?

The reason this enormous, innumerable group of people before the throne is commonly interpreted to be a group of martyrs beheaded during the day of the Lord's wrath, or "tribulation martyrs," is due to a phrase in Revelation 7:14. In his vision, John was speaking with one of the 24 elders, who offered him a chance to understand who these people were. When John admitted he did not know who they were, the elder provided the following explanation:

> So I said to him, "My lord, you know the answer." Then he said to me, "These are the ones

who have come out of the great tribulation [*tēs thlípseōs tēs mégalēs*]. They have washed their robes and made them white in the blood of the Lamb! (*Rev 7:14*)

This verse has caused a great deal of confusion with respect to the chronological flow of Revelation chapter 4 through 7. The traditional interpretation is that this enormous group of people is seen in soul-state under the altar during the opening of the fifth seal where each one is given a white robe, then in Revelation chapter 7, the group is seen before the throne. Still in their white robes, which they had to make white by enduring the beast, his image, and his mark, they came out of "the great tribulation." In order for this idea to be viable, the chronology of Revelation is "fast-forwarded," so to speak, such that this Revelation chapter 7 group is said to be killed by the beast, and then come out of the great tribulation. This even before the beast and his image are introduced within the Revelation chronology. In my view, this interpretation leaves much to be desired and is inconsistent with the basic chronology of the visions of Revelation.

The Greek phrase for "the great tribulation" in Revelation 7:14 is *tēs thlípseōs tēs mégalēs*. The Greek noun *thlípsis* is the key word that needs to be explored. Throughout the New Testament, *thlípsis* is translated many ways within the KJV. It is a noun which can be translated several ways in English, including "tribulation," "suffering," and "persecution." In the following table, a list of English words in the New Testament translated from the Greek word *thlípsis* is provided, along with examples of each usage in the KJV.

KJV English Word	Number of Usages	Examples of KJV Usages of *Thlipsis*
Tribulation	21	Behold, I will cast her into a bed, and them that commit adultery with her into great tribulation [*mégalen thlípsin*], except they repent of their deeds. (*Rev 2:22*) For then shall be great tribulation [*mégale thlípsis*], such as was not since the beginning of the world to this time, no, nor ever shall be. (*Mat 24:21*)
Affliction	17	Now there came a dearth over all the land of Egypt and Canaan, and great affliction [*mégale thlípsis*]: and our fathers found no sustenance. (*Act 7:11*)
Trouble	3	For we would not, brethren, have you ignorant of our trouble [*thlipseos*] which came to us in Asia, that we were pressed out of measure, above strength, insomuch that we despaired even of life: (*II Cor 1:8*)
Afflicted	1	Then shall they deliver you up to be afflicted [*thlípsin*], and shall kill you: and ye shall be hated of all nations for my name's sake. (*Mat 24:9*)
Anguish	1	A woman when she is in travail hath sorrow, because her hour is come: but as soon as she is delivered of the child, she remembereth no more the anguish [*thlípseos*], for joy that a man is born into the world. (*Joh 16:21*)
Burdened	1	For I mean not that other men be eased, and ye burdened [*thlípsis*]: (*II Cor 8:13*)
Persecution	1	Now they which were scattered abroad upon the persecution [*thlípseos*] that arose about Stephen traveled as far as Phoenicia, and Cyprus, and Antioch, preaching the word to none but unto the Jews only. (*Act 11:19*)

While many English words are used, just one Greek word is used in each case. One could question how the KJV translators knew when to use those different words, and when not to. When should "tribulation" be used? When should "anguish" be used? When should "affliction" be used? When should "trouble" be used? Of course, it depends on the context in which the word is used, but scanning over these verses, it seems that these words could be used interchangeably in each context without any harm to the meaning of the text. What if the usage in Matthew 24:21, instead of "great tribulation," was instead translated as "great suffering" or "great affliction?" Would the popular phrase "The Tribulation Period" instead be "The Affliction Period?" What about "The Great Burden" in place of "The Great Tribulation?"

One of the verses above, Acts 7:11, has the same Greek phrase, *mégale thlípsis*, as Matthew 24:21, and yet it was translated as "great affliction." So, why was this phrase not translated as "great tribulation" in the KJV as it was in Matthew 24:21, Revelation 2:22, and Revelation 7:14? What if the elder had told John that the enormous group just came out of "great anguish" or "great affliction" instead of "great tribulation?" Interestingly, in Mark's parallel passage to Matthew 24:21, the Greek *thlípsis* is again used, but the KJV translates it as "affliction" rather than "tribulation:"

> For then shall be great tribulation [*thlípsis*], such as was not since the beginning of the world to this time, no, nor ever shall be. (*Mat 24:21*)

> For in those days shall be affliction [*thlípsis*], such as was not from the beginning of the creation which God created unto this time, neither shall be. (*Mar 13:19*)

Why would the KJV translate two parallel passages, Matthew 24:21 and Mark 13:19, with two different English words when the underlying Greek words are identical? Again, these different English words can be used interchangeably to describe the same meaning, and these verses are absolute proof of that.

Bible commentators after the Protestant Reformation agreed that *tēs thlípseōs tēs mégalēs* of Revelation chapter 7 probably refers not to a particular time of trouble, but to great trial and anguish experienced during the life of every faithful member of the body of Christ, which anguish will be left behind. In his *Notes on the Bible* for Revelation 7:14, Albert Barnes noted, "The word rendered 'tribulation'–*thlípsis*–is a word of general character, meaning 'affliction,' though perhaps there is here an allusion to persecution. The sense, however, would be better expressed by the phrase great trials." John Wesley agreed that the massive group before the throne must be all the righteous since the beginning of the world when he wrote in his *Explanatory Notes* for Revelation 7:14, "...as all the angels appear here, so do all the souls of the righteous who had lived from the beginning of the world."

The point is that prophetic commentators have coined phrases such as "the tribulation period" and "the great tribulation," when these phrases could just as easily have been translated using different English words. If this were the case, then the "great tribulation" of Revelation 7:14 may have never been equated by default with a time of "great tribulation" prophesied by Jesus simply due to the use of popular eschatological lingo within the English language. The Greek phrase *tēs thlípseōs tēs mégalēs* deserves to be properly studied so that the correct meaning, free from unwarranted translative influence, can be brought to light.

The Narrow Path to Eternal Life

There is no exemption from persecution, suffering, or affliction for disciples of Jesus Christ. Rather, they are especially subject to it as their testimony among this present dark world is met by opposition. This is something Jesus made expressly manifest to his disciples on numerous occasions. While promising them peace in him through the Holy Spirit, he told them that in the world they would have trouble and suffering:

> I have told you these things so that in me you may have peace. In the world you have trouble and suffering [*thlipsis*], but take courage — I have conquered the world. (*Joh 16:33*)

Jesus again warned them in Matthew 24:9 that, during the time of the birth pains leading up to the end, they would be afflicted (*thlipsis*), hated, and killed. That the early church and the apostles experienced this type persecution is certainly confirmed in the New Testament. In Acts 11:19, Luke refers to a persecution (*thlipsis*) of the church resulting from the stoning of Stephen that scattered them into Phoenicia, Cyprus, and Antioch. Throughout his epistles, Paul constantly referred to his tribulations, sufferings, and afflictions, reminding his readers that the *thlipsis* he underwent was working patience in him, and were actually cause to rejoice. Though persecution and trouble were on every side, he was not crushed or dismayed. When Paul and Barnabas were traveling through Asia Minor, they strengthened the souls of the disciples at the churches in Lystra, Iconium, and Antioch of Pisidia by telling them that the entrance into the kingdom of God would be through "many persecutions (*thlipsis*)." Could this be what the elder was referring to when he told John that the innumerable group before the throne had come through great *thlipsis*?

In Revelation, John confirmed this idea by stating that, as a member of the kingdom of God, he was suffering persecution, and this persecution was shared by the seven churches of Asia:

> I, John, your brother and the one who shares with you in the persecution [*thlipsis*], kingdom, and endurance that are in Jesus, was on the island called Patmos because of the word of God and the testimony about Jesus. (*Rev 1:9*)

Some may be puzzled by the notion that the kingdom of God is entered through much persecution. The modern climate for Christianity is one of ecumenical, seeker-friendly amalgamation with the world and its modes of belief and entertainment. Has the Word of God changed, or has the church strayed from the Word to be friends with the world? Rather than question whether persecution is a proof that one is in the kingdom of God, one should question whether he is even a member of the kingdom of God if he is not experiencing persecution, according to these passages.

Both Strong's Lexicon and Thayer's Greek-English Lexicon of the New Testament define the Greek *thlipsis* as pressure applied to someone or something. *Thlipsis* comes from the root word *thlibō*, which means to be compressed, pressured, or constricted. One explanation used by Thayer for *thlibō* was how grapes are pressed in order to produce wine. Consider this passage:

> "Enter through the narrow gate, because the gate is wide and the way is spacious that leads to destruction, and there are many who enter through it. But the gate is narrow and the way is difficult [*tethlimméne*] that leads to life, and there are few who find it. (*Mat 7:13-14*)

The famous "straight and narrow" passage features Jesus' explanation of the broad path that leads to destruction and the narrow, constricted path that leads to life. The Greek *tethlimméne*, from the base verb *thlíbō*, is used to describe the way that leads to life. Jesus meant that he was the only way to eternal life, not one of many in a broad array of man's imaginations of how to inherit eternal life. The path is narrow and constricted–there is only one way. Is it possible that this is what the elder meant when he told John that the enormous group before the throne came out of *tēs thlipseōs tēs mégalēs*? That they had made their way down the constricted path that leads to life, coming out of the suffering of the present evil age? Based on these passages, it is a strong possibility that this is what the elder meant.

The Anguish of Childbirth
Jesus compared the pain and anguish a woman experiences during childbirth to the sorrow that the disciples would experience. As shown above, the Greek *thlípsis* was used to describe this anguish:

> When a woman gives birth, she has distress because her time has come, but when her child is born, she no longer remembers the suffering [*thlipseōs*] because of her joy that a human being has been born into the world. So also you have sorrow now... (*Joh 16:21-22*)

Paul also related the pain and groaning that life in this world brings, but also acknowledged that all of creation has been groaning and suffering together until the present time:

> For we know that the whole creation groans and suffers together until now. Not only this, but we ourselves also, who have the firstfruits of the Spirit, groan inwardly as we eagerly await our

adoption, the redemption of our bodies. (*Rom 8:22-23*)

The end of the groaning will come with the "redemption of our bodies," a direct reference to the resurrection of the dead, when mortal bodies are changed into immortal. So, not only does the whole of creation groan and suffer, but believers in Christ groan in anticipation of the transformation of their bodies.

Isaiah's prophecy of the redemption of our bodies provides a solid foundation for this interpretation. He foresaw a group, "my people," who will be hidden from the angry judgment of the Lord. In order for that group to be hidden from the judgment, they will have to be removed from the anguish on the earth. Isaiah described the anguish out of which they came using the metaphor of the pains of childbirth:

> As when a pregnant woman gets ready to deliver and strains and cries out because of her labor pains, so were we because of you, O Lord. We were pregnant, we strained, we gave birth, as it were, to wind. We cannot produce deliverance on the earth; people to populate the world are not born. (*Isa 26:17-18*)

The entire passage is full of metaphors about the suffering experienced when giving birth. The prophet compared the straining and crying of labor to the affliction of the people on the earth. The people declared that, despite all their straining, and even successful childbirth, they were unable to produce "deliverance on the earth." Although Israel strained to deliver a child, it was outside of their power. Only the Lord could produce that deliverance. Just after the allusion to the pains of childbirth, the prophet described two separate events that occur after the childbirth, but *before* the unleashing of the angry judgment of

143

the Lord upon the earth, avenging the shed blood on the earth. First, the resurrection of the dead, and second, the hiding away of all believers before the commencement of judgment, and until the judgment is over. The entire Isaiah 26:17-21 passage supports the idea that Christians first experience suffering and pain in this present world, but then come out of that great time of suffering by being instantly glorified and brought into the presence of the Lord. The *mégalēs thlípsis*, or anguish, experienced on earth with increasing frequency of contractions until the delivery, is left behind. The chosen remnant will leave the great pressures and persecutions of mortal life behind and be suddenly caught up, standing before the heavenly throne of God.

Therefore, rather than a specific time period in the future referring to the day of the Lord's wrath, *tēs thlipseōs tēs mégalēs* out of which an enormous, innumerable crowd of people will come, is reference to the life of the believer. Christians are called out to be separate, not of this world, and strangers and aliens on the earth. Jesus Christ promised that his faithful disciples would experience *thlípsis* while on the earth, but Paul said that *thlípsis* should be considered light in comparison to the eternal weight of glory that any physical and emotional suffering may be producing.

While all resurrected and caught up believers are standing before the throne in Revelation chapter 7, the earth is left to recover in the aftermath of the disaster of the sixth seal. After that disaster, the wrath of God will be poured out on the earth in the form of the trumpet judgments. However, before those judgments can begin, the seventh seal must be broken. The breaking of the final seal of the scroll results in a paradigm shift, a fusion of the dimensional realms of heaven and earth. A mysterious ceremony of incense at the golden altar by the high priest of heaven will accomplish this paradigm shift and result in the unleashing of the wrath of God on the earth.

144

11

AWAITING THE CEREMONY OF INCENSE

With the breaking of the seventh and final seal, the contents of the scroll are finally revealed: the wrath of God in the form of the trumpet and bowl judgments. This marks a paradigm shift both on the earth and in heaven. The earth will be reacting to the events of the sixth seal, realizing that the day of the Lord's wrath has come, but unprepared for the unparalleled destruction about to take place.

Prior to this paradigm shift, four spirits symbolized by riders on horses were granted permission to carry out an agenda of oppression and suffering on the earth through the events of the first four seals. After the shift, the supernatural realm begins to encroach on the realm of the natural world. But before the trumpet and bowl judgments can begin, the high priest of heaven will solemnly execute the ceremony of incense on the golden altar.

The Mysterious Activities at the Golden Altar of Incense

After a thirty minute silence, seven angels are given seven trumpets, but do not begin to blow them until certain activities at the altar of incense are carried out. A messenger is seen standing before the altar of incense, the same altar under which the souls of the martyrs cry out for vengeance during the fifth seal. When the seventh seal was opened in the vision, John saw the following:

> Another angel [*ággelos*] holding a golden censer [*libanōton chrusoun*] came and was stationed at the altar. A large amount of incense [*thumíamata polla*] was given to him to offer up, with the prayers of all the saints, on the golden altar that is before the throne. The smoke coming from the incense, along with the prayers of the saints, ascended before God from the angel's hand. Then the angel took the censer, filled it with fire from the altar, and threw it on the earth, and there were crashes of thunder, roaring, flashes of lightning, and an earthquake. (*Rev 8:3-5*)

John saw a solemn and powerful scene in heaven. A messenger began to offer incense, which represented the prayers of all the righteous ones, on the golden altar. The incense offered in this case is frankincense, an English word derived from the old French phrase *franc encens*, meaning "pure incense." The Greek *libanos* from which *libanōton* is derived simply means frankincense, and in this case, the golden censer is actually a fire pan specifically used for this pure heavenly frankincense. When frankincense powder is burnt, it emits a sweet fragrance. The messenger, therefore, is burning the prayers of the martyrs on the altar that is before the Lord, and the scent proceeded up to the Lord. John saw smoke from the burnt incense ascend from the altar of incense up to the throne of God. As the prayer incense is burnt, the ashes would fall into the coals of fire. Then, the messenger collected fiery coals from the altar in the golden censer and threw it onto the earth.

This passage closely parallels the Lord's instruction to Moses in Leviticus chapter 16 for the yearly procedure on the Day of Atonement. The high priest was to wash himself, put on holy garments, and enter the Most Holy Place. But before the yearly sacrifice offering of animals, the high priest was to offer incense:

> and take a censer full of coals of fire from the altar before the Lord and a full double handful of finely ground fragrant incense, and bring them inside the veil-canopy. (*Lev 16:12*)

Notice the similarities between what John saw and the Leviticus account: both refer to a censer, both take place before the altar, and both refer to incense. Next, the incense was to be placed on the fire:

> He must then put the incense on the fire before the Lord, and the cloud of incense will cover the atonement plate which is above the ark of the testimony, so that he will not die. (*Lev 16:13*)

Just as the smoke from the incense came before the throne of God in John's description, so the cloud of the incense covered the atonement plate in the passage from Leviticus, which is the Mercy Seat covering the Ark of the Covenant. Also note that in both passages, fire from the altar is mixed with the incense. The two passages are nearly identical up to this point.

Who is the messenger, or angel, carrying out these mysterious high priestly activities at the heavenly golden altar just before the sounding of the seven trumpet judgments? According to Hebrews chapter 9, the high priest of the new covenant is Jesus

Christ. The Greek *aggelos*, translated as "angel," is a word not restricted only to an "angel" interpretation. Its primary meaning is that of a messenger who is to announce or perform something. John the Baptist was referred to as an *aggelos* by Jesus:

> This is the one about whom it is written: 'Look, I am sending my messenger [*aggelos*] ahead of you, who will prepare your way before you.' (*Mat 11:10*)

In the context of the Revelation chapter 8 passage under consideration, the duties being carried out by this *aggelos* clearly match those performed by the high priest of heaven. Therefore, the messenger standing at the altar in verse 3 above must be Jesus Christ, the high priest, who has opened the seventh seal and is preparing to unleash the trumpet judgments on the earth.

By comparing the Revelation chapter 8 passage with the passage in Leviticus chapter 16, it is clear that the trumpet judgments could not be unleashed from heaven *until* the ceremonial activity at the altar with the incense and fire had been completed. The souls of the martyrs were constantly before the Lord, positioned underneath the altar of incense. They were crying out for vengeance, and their requests were collected in golden bowls. According to Revelation 8:3, a "large amount" of frankincense (*thumiamata polla* in Greek) was presented to Jesus for offering on the altar. Therefore, Jesus was actually offering up requests for vengeance from the martyrs that had for so long been positioned underneath the altar before the Lord. Once the smoke of the pure frankincense came up before the throne of God, he acknowledged the request of the martyrs for vengeance against those who shed their blood on the earth.

The importance of the burning of the incense in Revelation chapter 8, therefore, is seen in that God's vengeance is *withheld* until Jesus Christ, the high priest, offers the requests for vengeance on the incense altar and the fragrant smoke proceeds up to him. Just as the tearing of the veil of the temple represented a new and living way opened up for believers to the throne of grace, so the offering of the incense by the high priest on the golden altar before the throne of God triggers the unleashing of the vengeance of the Lord. No longer will the vengeance be withheld, and the seven angels will then be allowed to begin blowing the trumpets they are given.

This means, of course, that the first seal cannot be what it has traditionally been taught to be by nearly all pre-millennial prophetic models: the beginning of a future "Apocalypse," or day of the Lord's wrath. The wrath within the trumpet and bowl judgments is withheld until the offering of incense, and therefore, the opening of the seals do not constitute any part of the day of the Lord's wrath of God. Instead, the first five seals are part of the progression of history from the first century until the present, and the sixth seal embodies the catastrophic resurrection and catching-up event.

Contrasts Which Evidence the Paradigm Shift

There are several telling contrasts between the events which occur with the opening of the seals and the events which result from the trumpet and bowl judgments. These contrasts serve to further firmly establish that the events represented in the seals are different from the events represented in the trumpet and bowl judgments. They also underscore the paradigm shift that takes place after the opening of the seventh seal and the offering of incense on the golden altar.

1. Jesus listed events identical to the events of the first five seals and called them "birth pains" *before* the end, but the events of the trumpets and bowls definitely occur *after* the day of God's wrath has begun.

Instead of restricting the advent of false Christ's, wars, famines, pestilence, persecution, and death of Christians as events during the day of the Lord's wrath, Jesus stated in Matthew 24:8 that they would be birth pains that take place before the end comes. To what "things" was Jesus referring? The exact things described in the seals. As a review, consider the following table, which compares what Jesus described in Matthew and Luke as signs *before* the end with the events of the first six seals.

Events of Seals One Through Six	Events of Matthew 24 & Luke 21
A spirit of false religion in the name of Christ sent to dominate the people (seal one).	Many will come in my name saying "I am the Christ"; many will be misled.
A spirit of violence, torture, and bloodshed is unleashed on the earth, so that people violently butcher one another (seal two).	Nation will rise against nation and kingdom against kingdom; wars and rumors of wars.
A spirit of economic bondage and oppression (seal three).	(no prediction)
A spirit of death, disease, and famine (seal four).	There will be famines and plagues in various places.
The murder of Christians for their testimony of the gospel (seal five).	You will be persecuted, and they will kill you; you'll be hated and put to death.
Earthquakes, movement of mountains and islands, and signs in the heaven (seal six).	There will be earthquakes; there will be terrifying sights and great signs from heaven.

These are all signs before the end, according to Jesus; the beginning of the birth pains of the end. The events of the first six seals therefore must, according to the words of Christ, occur *before* the day of the Lord's wrath. Jesus described them as the beginning of the birth pains, and in the first century, they began to occur. As time has gone by, the contractions have begun to come faster and faster with more wars, more death, more disease, more famine, and more religious domination and deception. These things must occur, with less and less time between the contractions, before the birth, the end of the age, and before the beginning of the day of the Lord's wrath.

In contrast, the events of the trumpet and bowl judgments will take place after the day of wrath has come. When the sixth seal is opened and the effects of that seal begin to take place on the earth and in the heavens, the survivors will declare the day of the Lord's wrath has come. After that declaration, the seventh seal will be opened, and the seven trumpet judgments will begin.

2. The first four seals involve spirits going out *in the earth* who are granted permission to influence and oppress humanity, whereas the trumpet and bowl judgments are carried out at God's command by the holy angels *in heaven.*

According to Zechariah chapter 6, the spirits symbolized within the horses of Zechariah's vision are granted permission to carry out their oppressive assignments in the earth. Reviewing three of the first four seals, it is clear that these symbolic riders are likewise given permission to carry out their assignments in the earth. However, when the trumpet and bowl judgments are examined, which definitely take place during the day of the Lord's wrath, a paradigm shift has suddenly taken place. After the opening of the sixth seal, Jesus Christ is seen at the altar, carrying out the Day of Atonement activities. Then, God's holy angels pour out the judgments on the earth from heaven beginning with the trumpets in Revelation chapter 8, and then the bowls in Revelation chapters 15 and 16:

> Now the seven angels holding the seven trumpets
> prepared to blow them. (*Rev 8:6*)

> Then I saw another great and astounding sign in
> heaven: seven angels who have seven final
> plagues (they are final because in them God's
> anger is completed). (*Rev 15:1*)

In both cases, seven holy angels in heaven pour out the
judgments from heaven. However, the spirits of the first four
seals were granted permission to go into the earth to oppress
humanity. This is a clear contrast between the opening of the
seals and the trumpet and bowl judgments.

3. The sixth seal results in a reaction of *humility* and fear of God
   by the people on the earth, while the judgments of the
   trumpets and bowls result in a reaction of *blasphemy* and
   rebellion against God.

When the people on the earth see the results of the opening of
the sixth seal, their reactions and declarations will show fear,
humility, and desperation that the day of wrath has come. To
question who is able to withstand the great day of the wrath of
the Lamb and the wrath of God is rhetorical in nature, the
obvious answer being that no one will be able to stand against it.
They cry out in fear for the rocks and mountains to fall on them
so that they can be hidden from the Lord and the Lamb. They
would rather die by having rocks fall on them than to experience
the wrath of the day of the Lord. However, note the reaction at
the conclusion of the trumpet and bowl judgments:

> The rest of humanity, who had not been killed by
> these plagues, did not repent of the works of their
> hands, so that they did not stop worshiping

demons and idols made of gold, silver, bronze, stone, and wood—idols that cannot see or hear or walk about. Furthermore, they did not repent of their murders, of their magic spells, of their sexual immorality, or of their stealing. (*Rev 9:20-21*)

They blasphemed the God of heaven because of their sufferings and because of their sores, but nevertheless they still refused to repent of their deeds. (*Rev 16:11*)

And gigantic hailstones, weighing about a hundred pounds each, fell from heaven on people, but they blasphemed God because of the plague of hail, since it was so horrendous. (*Rev 16:21*)

Clearly there is a contrast between the reaction of humanity after these judgments during the day of the Lord's wrath, and their reaction to the sixth seal events before the day of the Lord's wrath had begun. Perhaps the "strong delusion" sent by God and referenced by Paul in II Thessalonians chapter 2, which causes unbelievers on the earth in the future who are deceived by the man of sin to believe what is false, is the reason for their rank rebellion during the trumpet and bowl judgments?

4. The events that take place within the opening of the first five seal judgments are all explained in the *natural* world and are currently taking place on the earth, whereas the trumpet and bowl judgments are *supernatural* in character, not seen currently in the earth.

Within the first five seals, there is the spirit of antichrist involving religious domination and oppression of humans in seal

153

one; war and bloodshed between humans in seal two; financial bondage and oppression of humans in seal three; death, disease, famine, and beasts of the earth wreaking havoc on one fourth of humanity in seal four; and martyrs suffering at the hand of other humans in seal five. The spirits of the first four seals are granted permission to carry out the oppression, but that oppression is carried out *through* natural means. The results can all be explained by natural or human causes, and are manifest in the world every day. These all occur prior to both the sixth seal events and the beginning of the day of the Lord's wrath.

This is in contrast to the supernatural events in trumpet and bowl judgments listed in the following table.

Judgment	Supernatural Events of the Trumpet Judgments	Supernatural Events of the Bowl Judgments
1	One-third of the entire earth will be burned, one-third of all the trees will be burned, and all the green grass will be burned due to hail with a fire and blood mixture.	Ugly and painful sores will appear on those who have the mark of the beast and who worship his image (this may be a natural reaction to the mark).
2	One-third of the sea will be turned to blood, one-third of all sea creatures will die, and one-third of all ships will be destroyed from a burning meteor object hitting the sea.	The sea will turn to blood, and all living creatures in the sea will die.
3	One-third of the rivers and springs will be turned bitter from being hit by a burning asteroid Wormwood.	All the rivers and springs will turn to blood.
4	The sun, moon, and stars are present in the skies one-third shorter time than normal.	The sun will become so hot that it will scorch people with fire and terrible heat.

Judgment	Supernatural Events of the Trumpet Judgments	Supernatural Events of the Bowl Judgments
5	Demonic locust-shaped creatures will ascend out of the bottomless pit and torture those who do not have the seal of God on their foreheads for five months. Men will not be able to die from their torment.	Darkness will cover the entire kingdom of the beast, and the darkness will cause pain for those in the kingdom.
6	Four angels will be loosed from the Euphrates River area, followed by two-hundred million beasts that breathe sulfur and will have snake-like tails that inflict injuries. These beasts will kill one-third of humanity with their smoke, fire, and sulfur.	The Euphrates River will dry up, and three evil spirits will proceed from the mouth of the dragon, the beast, and the false prophet to deceive the nations.
7	(none)	Earthquakes will cause all the cities of the earth to collapse, mountains to fall, and islands to be covered. In addition, 100 pound hailstones will hit the earth and its inhabitants.

Supernatural activity will encroach on the natural world as the veil is dissolved separating the spirit world from our current three-dimensional world. Blood and fire from heaven, disturbances in the reliable orbits of the heavenly bodies, spirits emerging from the abyss, and otherworldly creatures will be unleashed in the trumpet judgments. The bowl judgments will feature blood, fire, darkness, evil spirits, and unprecedented global destruction. The contrasts between the opening of the seals and these judgments are clear, and bolster an already strong case that the events of the first five seals are evident in the natural world, and will continue until the events of the sixth seal and the beginning of the day of the Lord's wrath.

The opening of the seventh seal will commence the unleashing of that wrath. The bridge between the events of the sixth seal catastrophe and the unleashing of the wrath of God will be the ceremony of fragrant pure incense on the golden altar before God's throne. Until then, the Lord's wrath is withheld, as he waits in patience for the men and women of the earth, created in his image, to turn from rebellion, make him Lord, and trust in him as Savior.

*   *   *

In conclusion, presented below is a summary of what I believe has taken place from the first century until the present, and what will unfold in the future, based on the catastrophic resurrection model detailed in this book.

1. Jesus Christ ascended to heaven and took his seat at the right hand of God in the first century. John was shown a vision of the first century ascension from a heavenly perspective so that we now understand the purpose for Jesus sitting down at the right hand of God: to take the scroll with seven seals and begin to break the seals. (Mar 16:19; Rev 5:1, 6-8, 6:1)

2. The 24 elders and the four living creatures, supernatural beings in the heavens, praised God and the Lamb with a "new song" when Jesus Christ appeared in heaven as the only one worthy to take the scroll from the right hand of God. (Rev 5:8-14)

3. The first four seals were broken by Jesus Christ in the first century just after his ascension to heaven and movement to sit down at the right hand of God. Spiritual entities symbolized in the first four seals were granted authority to

influence and oppress mankind from the first century until the present. (Rev 6:1-8)

4. The fifth seal martyrs represent believers killed throughout the centuries to the present, who are positioned underneath the throne of God. Their cries are heard constantly by the Lord near the altar of incense. In the future, the full number of martyrs will be reached with the murder of the final pre-sixth seal believers. (Rev 6:9-11)

5. The resurrection of the dead in Christ will take place at the opening of the sixth seal. The power of the resurrection of the dead into immortal bodies, in concert with the sounding of the "last trumpet," the voice of the Lord, will once more shake the earth. (I The 4:16-17; I Cor 15:51-53; Isa 26:19-20; Heb 12:26)

6. The bodies of both the resurrected dead in Christ and the living and remaining believers will be transformed into immortal, glorified bodies. (I Cor 15:51-53; Phi 3:20-21)

7. All believers will be suddenly caught up in transformed immortal bodies into the air to meet the Lord. (I The 4:16-17; Isa 26:19-20)

8. In a visit to Mount Sinai in Arabia just after his conversion, Paul met the Lord and was shown the mysteries he revealed in his epistles, including a pattern of the future resurrection of the dead in Christ and catching-up event. (Gal 1:13-17, 4:25; Exo 19:9-20)

9. The sixth seal events will be unleashed on the earth, including the movement of all mountains and islands, a massive earthquake, signs in the sun, moon, and sky, and possible magnetic or crustal pole shift. (Rev 6:12-14)

10. The earth will be devastated by the events of the sixth seal. Its survivors will attempt to make order out of chaos in a spirit of unification and with a vow to rebuild. Both Jesus and Paul prophesied the coming of the Lord would be

ushered in with a sudden destruction. (Luk 21:34-36, 17:23-30; I The 5:2-3)

11. Jesus compared his lightning-flash future appearance to two historic destructive events: the flood in the days of Noah and the destruction of Sodom in the days of Lot. Both events featured an unprepared world and sudden destruction. (Luk 17:24-37)

12. The day of the Lord's wrath will begin on the earth, according to the declaration of the people on the earth, after the sixth seal events. (Rev 6:16-17, 16:5-6; Isa 26:21)

13. The enormous and innumerable group of believers before the throne of God represent the resurrected, transformed, and caught-up believers on the earth, escaping the devastation of the events of the sixth seal on the earth. They came through the "great tribulation" or persecution of life on the earth, and made their robes white by putting their trust in the shed blood of Jesus Christ. (Rev. 7:9-14; Luk 21:36)

14. The ceremony at the altar of incense will commence, with the seventh and final seal being opened. The scroll contained in those seven seals, written on front and back, detail the seven trumpet judgments on one side and the seven bowl judgments on the other. (Rev 5:1, 8:1-5)

15. The judgments of the trumpets and bowls will serve to cleanse a defiled earth of the shedding of innocent blood. The cry of the martyrs throughout the ages for vengeance for the shedding of their innocent blood will be answered with these judgments. (Rev 6:9-11, 16:5-7; Isa 26:20-21)

While this marks the end of this prophetic model, it should not mark the end of the study of the connections between the trumpet of God, the resurrection of the dead, and the events of the sixth seal. I encourage you to continue to study the Word of God, like the Bereans of Acts 17:11, to "see if these things are so."

EPILOGUE

REQUIEM FOR POST-MODERN ATHEISM

In the post-modern world in which we currently live, the Sovereign God of the Bible has been denigrated due to the considerable influence of a persuasive and well-orchestrated intelligentsia. Atheistic public schools, colleges and universities, now the breeding grounds for all forms of sexual decadence and abuse of mind-altering substances, are also sanctuaries for the exaltation of naturalistic evolution over the supernatural truths in the Bible. There is no absolute truth, they boldly proclaim; rather, all truth is relative. My truth does not have to be someone else's truth, but rather, truth is based on what I feel in my heart to be true. If your truth is found in the Bible, that may be great for *you*, but it does not represent *my* truth. The moral relativist does not make room in their worldview for the existence of a God who proscribes how one must conduct oneself. However, there are two absolute proofs of the existence of God that cannot be refuted by post-modern moral relativists, agnostics, or atheists.

The first is the fulfillment of Bible prophecy. The overriding purpose of the prophetic scriptures is not to quench the human thirst to know what is going to happen in the future, as if the Lord were somehow obliged to provide it. Rather, the main purpose of the prophetic scriptures is to prove that there is a God who spoke to men whom he appointed as prophets, who in turn obediently recorded what the Lord told them. Fulfillment of the events embodied within these recorded words foretold hundreds of years in advance, with 100% accuracy, is proof that there must be an all-knowing, all-powerful God who was the source of the inspiration of those prophetic words.

Second, the mere existence of Jesus Christ as a historical figure is proof of the existence of God, because he claimed to be God and backed up those claims with omnipotence. The supernatural power and authority he displayed over the human body, the spirit world, the natural world, and the grave prove that his claims of equality with God were absolutely true. He also backed up the claim to be God by displaying qualities of omniscience, such as during his encounter with the Samaritan woman at Jacob's well (Joh 4:1-30) and by prophesying of future events that came to pass with the destruction of the temple in Jerusalem (Mat 24:1-2). External, objective realities cannot be internally, subjectively denied.

Therefore, the arguments against the existence of God will no longer be tolerated. While Friedrich Nietzsche long ago proclaimed the death of God and his humanistic disciples have reveled in that fantasy ever since the rebellious proclamation, I, through the empty tomb of Jesus Christ and the eyewitnesses to his resurrection, hereby proclaim *the truth*: God the Father is very much alive, with his Son Jesus Christ at his right hand. In order to facilitate the fantasy that "God is dead," they sacrifice undeniable, objective truth on the Altar of Skepticism. At the root of the rebellious Nietzchean fantasy is pride: the inability and unwillingness to submit to the inherent authority of a sovereign God, desiring rather to independently determine their own fate and to be the ruler of their own domain.

Because Jesus Christ is equal with God (Phi 2:6) and created all persons (Joh 1:1-9), he has inherent sovereign authority over all humanity and the universe. This means you and I must surrender to the authority of Jesus Christ. It is one thing to *call* him Master and Lord with your mouth, and quite another to *make* him the Master and Lord of your words, thoughts, and actions by obeying his commands in complete humility. He cannot be your Savior unless he is first your Master and Lord. If you have a problem with the idea of a Sovereign God ruling over your thoughts and actions, then you must question whether you are truly a disciple of Jesus Christ.

Jesus Christ is King of Kings, seated at the right hand of the throne of God, and has all authority and power. As the righteous judge of mankind, his kingdom stands eternally opposed to sin and rebellion. Just as an inventor has the inherent rights to an invention or an author holds the copyright for a book he has written, so the Lord has the inherent rights to the earth he created and everyone in it. Because he holds the patent to the creation, he has the right to demand how it is used and how we interact and conduct ourselves within it. If that omnipotence and omniscience were the only reason to worship and obey him, it would be enough. But he not only created the world and everyone in it, he also became one of us, and willingly offered himself to be butchered and crucified by his own creation in order to provide for its salvation.

How could I not bow in reverence and amazement to a King such as this? Earthly kings desire power, wealth, and fame, but this King desires mercy, servanthood, and sacrifice. This King humbled himself below all of his subjects in order to save them from their sins. Instead of giving me justice and crushing me back into dust, he vowed to save me in his boundless mercy. In the ultimate of paradoxes, God used my murder of his Son to be the medium by which I am saved! On the cross, the sinless Lamb became a curse so that a sinful human being like yourself could have his righteousness credited to your account by trusting in his blood atonement for forgiveness. Without the shedding of blood, there can be no remission of your sins, and you remain a magnet of the wrath of God. But the perfect, sinless blood of Jesus Christ can remit the sin of every person who repents and trusts in his sacrifice.

Every knee will bow and acknowledge his authority, because he has earned the right to rule and receive all glory and honor through his perfect sacrifice and resurrection from the dead. Come to him in humility, understanding the quantum lengths to which he descended in order to become a human being and experience a gruesome, excruciating death at your bloody hands. Put your trust in his sacrificial atonement for your acts of rebellion against him, realizing his perfect existence was crediting to your sinful account. Believe the eyewitnesses of his resurrection from the dead and ascension to heaven. Then, pick up a cross daily in gratitude, obey his commandments in the Word of God with joy, and follow him without wavering, no matter the price.

SELECTED BIBLIOGRAPHY

Cornuke, Robert (2000). *In Search of the Mountain of God: The Discovery of the Real Mt. Sinai.* Nashville: Broadman and Holman Publishers.

Goodgame, Peter D. (2005). *Red Moon Rising: The Rapture and the Timeline of the Apocalypse.* Longwood, Florida: Xulon Press.

Griffin, G. Edward (1998, Third Edition). *The Creature from Jekyll Island: A Second Look at the Federal Reserve.* Westlake Village, California: American Media.

Hengel, Martin (1961). *The Zealots: Investigations into the Jewish Freedom Movement in the Period from Herod I until 70 A.D.* Edinburgh: Clark.

Habermas, Gary R. and J.P. Moreland (1992). Immortality: The Other Side of Death. Nashville: Thomas Nelson Publishers.

Hoehner, Harold W. (1977). Chronological Aspects of the Life of Christ. Grand Rapids, Michigan: Zondervan Publishing House.

Hunt, Dave (1994). *A Woman Rides the Beast*. Eugene, Oregon: Harvest House Publishers.

Lowe, David (2005). *Earthquake Resurrection: Supernatural Catalyst for the Coming Global Catastrophe*. Morrisville, North Carolina: Lulu Press.

Metzger, Bruce M. (1993). *Breaking the Code: Understanding the Book of Revelation*. Nashville: Abingdon Press.
Möeller, Dr. Lennart (2002). *The Exodus Case: New Discoveries Confirm the Historical Exodus*. Copenhagen: Scandinavia Publishing House.

Möeller, Dr. Lennart (2002). The Exodus Case: New Discoveries Confirm the Historical Exodus. Copenhagen, Denmark: Scandinavia Publishing House.

Moorehead, William G. (1908). Studies in the Book of Revelation. Pittsburgh: United Presbyterian Board of Publication.

Mounce, Robert H. (1977). *The New International Commentary on the New Testament: The Book of Revelation*. Grand Rapids, Michigan: William B. Eerdman's Publishing Company.
Patten, Donald W. (1988). *Catastrophism and the Old Testament: The Mars-Earth Conflicts*. Seattle: Pacific Meridian Publishing Company.

Tipler, Frank J. (1994). *The Physics of Immortality*. New York: Doubleday.

Walvoord, John F. (1990). *The Prophecy Knowledge Handbook*. Wheaton, Illinois: Scripture Press Publications, Inc.

164

Wilson, Ian (1986). *The Mysterious Shroud.* New York: Doubleday.

Wilson, Ian (1998). *The Blood and the Shroud.* New York: The Free Press.

ALSO AVAILABLE FROM SEISMOS PUBLISHING

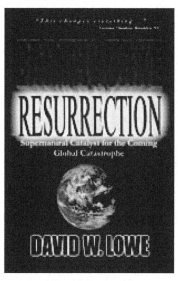

Earthquake Resurrection

Supernatural Catalyst for the Coming Global Catastrophe

ISBN: 1-4116-3970-7

"The most logical, well-referenced, understandable, and convincing explanation of end-times prophecy I have ever heard or read."

– David Adams

Earthquake Resurrection features a detailed exploration of a resurrection of the dead to immortality and its association with a shaking of the earth. What impact will the power of the simultaneous resurrection of millions of people in a single moment have on the physical structure of the earth? Startling new biblical evidence is presented to support the belief that the future disappearance of believers in the rapture will discounted as "missing persons" amidst the greatest global catastrophe since the Flood of Noah.

"David achieves the near impossible: After 2,000 years of analysis and debate of apocalyptic prophecy, Earthquake Resurrection manages to offer a fresh take on the events of the End Times."

– Derek P. Gilbert, PID Radio

Deconstructing Lucifer

Reexamining the Ancient Origins of the
Fallen Angel of Light

ISBN: 978-0-6155-3386-5

I have just finished reading Deconstructing Lucifer for the second time. Just wanted you to know that it was the most insightful and informative book I have read in the past 10 years.

– Larry Cross, *Freedom From Delusion* blog

Have you ever wondered where the story of the fall of Lucifer originated? Was Satan really once a beautiful heavenly angel named Lucifer? Did God cast Lucifer out of heaven because he was filled with pride? Did Satan lead an ancient rebellion of one third of the angels against God?

Deconstructing Lucifer delves deep into the history of the story of Lucifer to answer these and many other questions about Satan and his origins. Investigate the earliest sources in order to determine who was responsible for the story of Lucifer and its ultimate adoption as a mainstream teaching. Hebrew, Greek, and Latin word studies will serve to illuminate the relevant passages of scripture for you, uncovering their proper meaning.

In the end, you will be equipped with answers to the toughest questions about the origin of Satan, the source of evil in the world, and the sovereignty of God in allowing them to exist.

In reconciling the idea that both Lucifer and Jesus could be the "morning star," for me personally, Deconstructing Lucifer was an answer for which I waited 10 years.

– Amos Ridley, *Truthstream Oasis* podcast

Made in the USA
Monee, IL
25 February 2021